CASH IN 30 DAYS!

A Quick Start Guide To Making Money
From Buying and Selling Houses.

Sandy Cesaire

COPYRIGHT

or service contained within the Third Party Material. Use of recommended Third Party Material does not guarantee that your results will mirror our own. Publication of such Third Party Material is simply a recommendation and expression of the authors' own opinion of that material.

Real estate investing contains risk like any other investments or business. Investors should proceed with caution. Investors can make or lose money on any given transaction. Great effort has been exerted to safeguard the accuracy of this writing. Opinions regarding the subject matter covered in this eBook have been formulated as a result of both personal experiences, as well as the experiences of others.

Books may be purchased by contacting the publisher and author at www.SandyCesaire.com

Publisher: Sandy Cesaire

Printed in the United States Of America

First Edition

ISBN: 978-0-615-97265-7

Table Of Contents

ACKNOWLEDGMENTS

- I would like to dedicate this book to my parents, Jules Cesaire and Marie Martin. You are my rock and my motivation. Thank you for all of your sacrifices.

- To my uncle Benito Martin, thank you for your faith and investment in me.

- To my sisters, Linda Esta and Roseline Jacques-Louis, thank you for your encouragements and for being the best big sisters a girl could ever ask for.

SPECIAL THANKS TO:

I would like to give a special thank you to the following awesome God-sent people for their continuous support and effort in helping me make my dreams a reality. Thank you for believing in me, and thank you so very much for everything that you've done for me.

Amani Channel

Andrew Collins

Morana St Hilaire

Leonard Marks

Ainsley Daux

ADDITIONAL THANKS TO:

To you all, Thank you for playing such a positive role in my life. You are always there when I need you. There aren't enough words to express how much I appreciate you. Thank you!

Clavel Jacques-Louis	Barbara Niswonger
Coles Mercier	Dolmar Cross
Peggy Edwards	William "Bill" Donovan
Andrew Ashmeade	George Scribano

I would also like to say a very special thank you to Vornholt. Thank you for your contribution and sharing your with my students.

You Don't Have To Be Broke No More!

Poem Written By: Sandy Cesaire

So you want to make money in real estate

But you don't know how to start or where to concentrate

Well put your thinking cap on and let us go through it

Are you dead broke, bankrupt with bad credit?

Or do you have a full time job and you need to part time it

Are you willing to do what it takes and be dedicated?

Learn the ropes, get educated

Minimize your risk but when an opportunity is presented

Will you learn to recognize it, evaluate it?

Drop your fear and grab it

Look around. By real estate you are surrounded

But, where's the deal...how can you find it?

Coach up, mentor up, read my book, learn how to spot it...

Let's face it!

You don't have to be broke no more, or bankrupted

The reality is you CAN make money investing in real estate

But first, I need you to change your broke mindset... let's
uncorrupt it

Then we can concentrate on setting you financially free

One property at a time, building a life you love...

A life YOU Have Created!

Introduction

All of your questions regarding investing in real estate can be answered through proper counsel, education and most important of all, experience.

"What do I need to do to in order to get started?" and "How can I get started making money in real estate?"

These are questions that people that are interested in the real estate investing business often ask me.

Have you asked anyone about how you can start making money investing in real estate lately; especially after seeing the success they are having with it? Maybe you've been thinking about getting started for awhile, but you don't have anyone to guide you. You may even have a full time job and are not sure how you would successfully fit a real estate business in your schedule part-time. Or, you could be battling with the premise that you would somehow screw up and fail, so you may find it hard to have the courage to just go for it.

I'm not sure what your personal reasons are for not getting started, but whatever they are, I hope I can help give you the push, as well as provide you with the resources that you need in order to get your real estate investing business up and running right away.

The main reason in writing this book is to answer these questions for you. If you are a person who has limited resources: little to no money, no credit, no access to cash, and no experience in real estate, then this book is specifically for you.

I wrote this book with your success in mind. Without The B.S.

This is a straightforward, step-by-step "real world" guide that you can begin to implement right now. Follow up for additional training and resources by visiting www.REICashIn30Days.com and the links to the other websites I provided throughout this book. After reading this entire book you will have all of the tools you need to start making money right away. There is more research for you to do, but I am going to get you off to a great start.

This book will change your life when you take massive action and implement the lessons you will learn here. I am sharing the same strategies I used that helped me get from damn near homelessness to making five figures monthly in just a matter of a couple of months by applying these strategies. I will teach you everything you need to get started.

If you are as serious as I am about helping you make a real difference in your life then understand that NOW is the time for you to Get Real and Get To Work! Not tomorrow, not in a few years, or when the kids gets older. When it comes to your life struggles and difficulties, I don't just want to help you put a bandage on to soothe things for the time being, I want to help you cure your financial wounds, once and for all. I want to help you achieve the success and financial freedom that you have been craving through smart real estate investing. I want to help you make your life great. Period!

In this book, I take a No B.S. approach in order to get you over that "beginner's hump", to get you to the other side where financial freedom awaits you. Now, I do not claim to "know it all", but if you pick up just ONE piece of information from me that gets you closer to your desired goal, then all of this will have been worth it for you. So let's get down to business.

Real Estate Investing Is Quite Simple

Making money in real estate is very simple once you learn the basic fundamentals of the business. Be resourceful and keep an open mind.

Real estate investing is not rocket science. If it were I would have been SOL! Thankfully (for both you and me), it's actually very simple. Have you ever dealt with anything that is complicated or just plain difficult? If you have, then I am sure you can totally respect the difference. The elements that make something "difficult" or "complicated" are entirely different, just as with "easy and simple".

The reason why I bring up "simple, easy, complicated, and difficult" is to illustrate to you why you should NOT be intimidated by the real estate investing business. It's not because I'm an expert on the topic of difficult and complicated... Well, at least don't ask my exes.

Real estate investing is so simple, just about anyone can do it. If I can do it, YOU certainly can too. However, I am not claiming that it is easy; although it CAN be, when you are willing to make sacrifices, form the right relationships, and put in the hard work that is required to get to achieve success. So keep reading.

Investigate Before You Invest

Investigate Before You Invest.

One of the elements that can make starting out in real estate difficult is the overabundance of different "tactics" and "investing methods" getting pumped out by these so-called "real estate gurus". Most of the time, these Gurus are simply taking investment strategies that have existed for a long time, and simply renaming them without changing anything about that strategy which confuses the beginning investor.

While experienced investors can see the trickery a mile away, new investors get confused and overwhelmed with repetitive information, only to end up giving up because they don't know what else to do. Today, you may find an article written about "the best investing strategy" to make money in real estate, only to see numerous articles telling you why that same strategy is dead and is no longer working in the market the following day. And all of this is ONLY because another "hot shot Guru" has started marketing "The NEW next best strategy" that worked for them.

So, as a beginner, you could end up wasting your time and money going in circles constantly bouncing from product to product, when you should be spending that time on "Income

Producing Activities". This means that you should be **FOCUSING ON SPECIFIC ACTIONS** that will actually get you Real Results, increase your chances of success in this business and make you real money.

Educating yourself is important but APPLYING what you learn is even more important.

Another major problem is that the majority of people that purchase products, DO NOT follow the lesson plans and DO NOT do the work it takes to see success. They DO NOT become successful simply because they DO NOT take action! These are the types of people that always want the easy "make money in your sleep" approach to everything. They will buy anything that tells them they don't have to put in work.

Marketers exploit and take full advantage of individuals with the 'lazy' mindset. They tell you what you "WANT" to hear. You are sold on their products with SEDUCTIVE headlines that remind you of your pains, pleasures and even your weakness. They use various marketing tactics to draw people in. And guess what? It WORKS!

Now, I'm not saying there is anything wrong with that, because if someone did create a product that can really benefit you and improve your life then they need to put it in front of you. You NEED to hear about it. But you have a responsibility to yourself to INVESTIGATE BEFORE YOU INVEST any of your money, time or energy into any products. Check out the credibility of the person who's teaching the material as well as the product. Some programs for example will allow you to do a 7 to 30 day test try to see if the program is a fit for you. Based on your own goals that you have set for yourself and your life; is this a product that's going to get you closer to achieving YOUR goals?

Only YOU can answer this question.

Investigate before you invest your hard earned money on any courses or products. Ask yourself, is this product a good fit for me? What value will this bring me?

Investigate before you invest. Don't be too anxious or too quick to hand over your hard earned money to get your hands on "The Next Best Thing" before you even take the time to check it out. Ask yourself; is this product a good fit for me? What value will it add to my life should I follow its course? How will I make back the money that I invested to get that education? How am I going to use the information I learn? How will this benefit me?

Make sure that you are spending your money and your time on products and training that will get you the results that you want. Everything is not for everybody. A product or a course that may be perfect for another person may not potentially be what you need. Don't be one of those people who are quick to buy a product because of the "hype" that surrounds it. Some people who are quick to complain when a product don't produce the results that they were expecting when in reality, they should have never invested their time, energy or money on a product that was not a good fit for them in the first place. You must investigate before you invest. You must know what your needs are before you start spending. For example, take inventory of what skills, techniques or strategies you need to learn in order to accomplish your goals. What tools do you need and if you have it and use it, will it take your business to the next level? Write down a list of things that you need in order to achieve the financial results that you are seeking. This can be tools, skills, equipment, training, personal coaching. Once you have this list, do not purchase any products that are not on that list, instead invest in marketing or generating more business so you can reach your financial goals.

On the flip side, there are many educational products that actually DO work when you take the time to implement the material you learn. When you invest your money into educational and training courses that have the potential to help you, don't set the material aside and do nothing, as if the information will miraculously seep into your brain and somehow create some action for you.

Chase The Rabbit You Are Sure To Catch

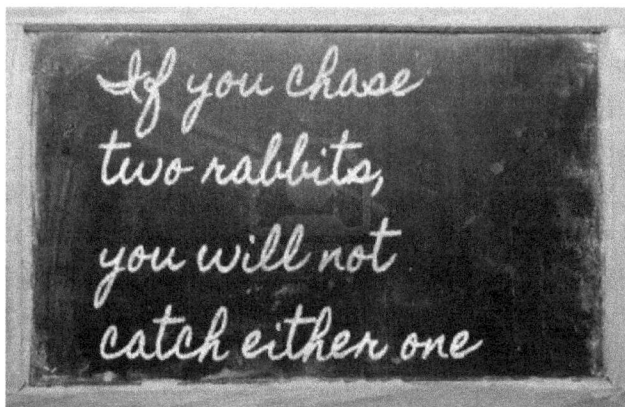

Focus, Focus, Focus on Income Producing Activities. If you don't you will never get anything done.

Since you are reading this book, it's likely you are serious about improving your life and your current financial situation. You may be looking for a way to bring in a few extra thousands of dollars into your household, or generate a second income. Or, it could be that you are interested in being your own boss, owning your own business, and having more control of your time. Working for yourself can give you that option. No matter what your reason for getting involved in the real estate business, first know that YOU CAN DO IT. It is very possible for you to run your own real estate investing business and make a lot of money doing it, but what you have got to do is STOP CHASING EVERYTHING THAT LOOKS GOOD!

There are countless ways you can make money investing in real estate. Figure out which method works for you, start with that and stick to it until you master it and profit from it.

There's an old proverb that says, "He who chases two rabbits catches none". So focus on learning the business, find out which 1 or 2 strategies will work best for you according to YOUR current situation, YOUR personal plan, and YOUR available resources. STOP chasing a bunch of different strategies. You can be productive chasing the dream but you will not be productive chasing the hype. Do Not Chase The Hype!

With that said, I'm going to teach you exactly what you need to do to get started making money in real estate within the next 30 to 45 days. But it will only happen if you take massive action and implement the techniques that I am going to teach you. Now I cannot make you any guarantees because your results will be a direct reflection of the quality of work and time you actually dedicate to building your business.

How To Get Started Making Money In Real Estate

Getting started is quite simple. All you have to do is Learn the business and Do The Work!

You do not need any other guru's products to get your first deal closed. Period! And if you're going to invest into anything at all, other than marketing, I suggest that you invest in a software program that can help you generate, track, market and analyze your real estate deals. After you have successfully closed a deal or two, then you can invest in more gadgets if you wish. Right now I want you to Keep It Short and Simple (K.I.S.S.), focus on the details I have laid out for you here, TAKE ACTION and DO THE DAMN WORK!

Feel free to purchase any other products that you want, I just want you to understand that it will only potentially confuse you, overwhelm you and slow down your progress. But, if you must purchase a course, remember to INVESTIGATE BEFORE YOU INVEST. Make sure it complements what you are already learning and doing, and it's not something that will take you off track and cause you to lose focus.

Now let's get to work. Take out your notepad or your IPad, and take notes. It's time to grind.

Before You Close Your First Deal

There are many ways to make money investing in real estate.

Just remember that in order to make money in this business, you have to close deals. You need to contract or buy properties that you can sell, or even if you want to generate a monthly cash flow, you need properties to rent, or owner-finance. So that means you need to focus ONLY on the activities that will generate that income for you, and avoid the pitfalls of time, energy and money wasting activities. This book is focused on buying and selling, real estate. I am going to show you exactly what you need to do to get your first offer made, get properties into your inventory and get deals to the closing table and put some cash in your pocket immediately and how to avoid the pitfalls most investors make..

To make money in your real estate investing business, there are a few things that you need to do:

1. You need to sell or rent properties.

1. In order to sell properties you are going to have to find the properties that you are going to sell.

2. You need to know how and where to locate these properties.

3. Furthermore, you need to know how to evaluate, negotiate and secure that deal once you find it.

4. You need to know how to successfully facilitate and complete a real estate transaction. (There is much that needs to happen between the time you place theproperty under contract and the time you close the deal.)

5. You need to know how and where to market the properties for sale. You need to know how to find buyers for these properties. For the purpose of this book, specifically cash buyers and investors who will buy from you over and over again.

6. You need education. Basically, you need to know how to do all of these things to

7. Make money and be successful or you need to have someone such as a coach or mentor that knows how to successfully complete a transaction to guide you.

My focus here is to teach you only the strategies and activities you need to know to start closing deals ASAP, with as minimal monetary investment from you as possible. This book is not about teaching you how to rehab, rent or any other strategies that will take a longer time period to make you money. You can get my other books for that. I'm going to show you the quickest way to make money in this business with very little to no cash by marketing properties that you either secure, or buy at huge discounts and quickly sell them to cash buyers and investors. However, you will have to learn to be resourceful, take the strategies that I'm teaching you and implement them.

I did not include money on the list of things you need to close a deal because the lack of funds is the least of your worries right now. Having money helps, but it is very possible to complete these transactions without using your own money and sometimes without using any money at all. You will see why throughout this book.

Real Estate Investing Is A Team Effort

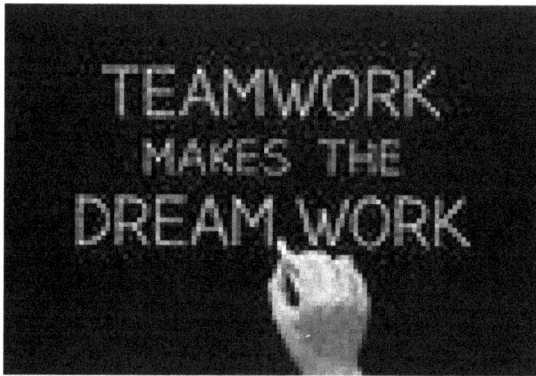

You will need help from other real estate professionals to successfully complete your transactions.

You need to put together a team of professionals that provide the services needed to get your transactions done. The types of professionals you will need on your team are:

Real Estate Agents

Real Estate Wholesalers

Real Estate Attorneys

Title Companies

Bird Dogs/House Hunters

Certified Public Accountants (CPA's)

General Contractors

Hard Money Lenders

Real Estate Appraisers

Insurance Agents

Property Inspectors

Handymen

Private Lenders

Mortgage Brokers

Personal Assistant

Project Managers

Property Managers

Coach or Mentor

As a newbie, you won't necessarily need all of these people right away. For example, you do not necessarily need a personal assistant, project manager, acquisition and/or sales manager to get started. However, if you're thinking of operating your business on a larger scale and developing a large sales team then you may need a property acquisition manager and sales manager but they are not a requirement when you are just getting started. As your business grows and you start making money, you can hire people to fulfill those positions.

A personal assistant can come in handy if you can afford one. An assistant can research information on properties for you in addition to numerous other tasks. This would allow you the time to focus on more income generating activities. If your budget does not allow for you to hire an assistant right away, that's fine. You don't need one up front to make money. You can always hire someone after you close a few deals, if you find that hiring an assistant will help you reach your goals.

Real Estate agents, title agents, and mortgage brokers get paid from the deals themselves when the transactions close. So you don't have to pay them any out-of-pocket money up-front. The title company normally disburses each person's funds after each deal closes and the money that funds the deal has cleared their account. On the contrary, appraisers, inspectors and insurance agents normally collect their fees up front; although they can also get paid at closing if you work those terms out with them in advance.

Keep in mind that everything in this business is negotiable so very few rules (including who pays for what) are set in stone. Since you are new to this business, you may not know people in these professions. It is for this reason, you MUST network and start to build relationships with others who are already in the real estate business so they can refer you to the best people that can and will help you.

Networking

Networking and building solid relationships with other professionals in this business is essential to your success.

The level of success you achieve in this business is dependent upon you building the right types of relationships with the right people. Networking will open the door for you to meet and connect with people that will give you access to all types of resources you will need to be successful in this business.

You can take several approaches to networking, but I am only going to focus on the networking techniques that will produce the best results for you in the shortest period of time. You first need to start by attending your local real estate investors (REIA) meetings. You can also take advantage of the networking opportunities through the use of social media platforms such as Facebook, LinkedIn, Twitter, and Google plus to name a few. There are also other online networking platforms such as meetup.com.

You need to start establishing relationships with wholesalers, all types of real estate investors, lenders, and other industry professionals such as mortgage brokers, real estate agents, general contractors, appraisers, etc. You must create valuable connections with the right people that can help you fill in the gaps, give you advice, and many resources that would otherwise be very difficult, costly and time consuming to get on your own.

Real Estate Investors Meetings

Find out where your local REIA (Real Estate Investor Association) meets, attend and network.

Before you go to look at any properties, the first thing you need to do is put yourself in an environment with other real estate investors. Find out where the local investor meetings are and start attending them. They all have different schedules. Some of them hold weekly meetings and others are held monthly. There are many real estate investor clubs throughout this country. You can find out where your local investment clubs meet on this website http://www.nationalreia.com. Do a Google search as well because there may be even more real estate investing groups that are not listed on that website. You can also visit my website for a detailed list of these real estate investor associations around the country.

There are several reasons why you must attend these meetings. The primary reason is to network with local investors that are currently ACTIVE in the business. They can introduce you to other real estate professionals that you will need various services from in order to get your deals done. Once you develop a relationship with these people, they may become a great resource for you. You may even be able to call them to ask for advice or assistance when you start working your own deals. This can be very valuable, especially when you come across obstacles and challenging deals. For this reason, it is important for you to make sure to focus on building solid relationships with investors who have a great deal of experience. It is also important to network with everyone, regardless of their level of experience, because even your fellow newbies could be potential buyers, sellers and a good source of leads for you. Make sure to network with everyone.

The other benefits of joining these real estate clubs and attending the meetings are the immense amount of education that you will get from them. The great news is that most of the education is FREE! You will learn many investing secrets and advanced techniques from guest speakers and industry experts at these meetings. Plus, as I mentioned before, there's a lot to be learned from the veteran members who have been investing in real estate for decades and frequent these meetings.

Finally, let's address the cost to attend the meetings. Each organization is different. Some of the investor's clubs charge a yearly membership fee to join the group and in return they offer tons of benefits to their members. However you don't necessarily have to be a member to attend the meetings. Just keep in mind; if you are not a member, you may have to pay a fee at the door to be a guest at the meeting. The fees that they charge vary from club to club. These investors clubs have cost involved to organize those meeting. Many of them have to pay for the venue where the meeting is held in addition to other cost. So it is only fair that they charge a fee to offset their cost. However, there are other investors clubs that meet at local restaurants, offices or other facilities. Some of those clubs do not charge a fee to attend. For example, if the meeting is taking place at a restaurant, you may not have to pay to attend, but in return you have to place an order from the restaurant for occupying their space. That is a small price to pay for the amount of valuable information and contact you get at these meetings; Information that can seriously put you on the right path to financial freedom.

Networking Through Social Media

Social media can be a powerful networking tool for the new investor if used right.

You can network with other real estate professionals on the Internet through social media. When done right, you can effectively grow your network and build relationships on these platforms. I get leads from social media daily because I actually engage and connect with people. After you start being more active and connecting with key people on these platforms, the same will happen for you.

Don't just create a profile on Facebook, Twitter, LinkedIn, or any of the others and then sit by and watch all of the action... Engage! Participate in the action! Join the real estate groups; interact with other people, and BE ACTIVE. You can use these platforms to share valuable and interesting information, and ask questions. The point is interact with others and **Be Active and Be Yourself**. Be respectful, but don't be shy. One thing to keep in mind is social media can be addictive so if you're going to be on it, remember to get off and GET TO WORK. Do not waste the hours and hours that you can use to put your deals together on social media reading gossip and nonsense. Gossip and nonsense don't pay unless you work for TMZ and the

National Enquirer so **Stay Productive and FOCUS ON MONEY MAKING ACTIVITIES.**

Create your profile on the social media platforms, join the real estate investment groups, engage and network.

There are so many social platforms available on the Internet nowadays. If you don't have an account with the top social networking sites, make sure you get one, and look for real estate groups to join so you can start networking with other investors immediately. To start, create a profile on www.facebook.com, and www.linkedin.com.

I personally have never gotten any leads from Twitter, and I am really just now getting comfortable with it, but I have friends that do great with Twitter, so check out www.twitter.com. Also check out http://www.Pinterest.com and http://www.Instagram.com as well. You can use platforms like Pinterest and Instagram to market yourself and post pictures of properties you are selling; you can use hashtags (#) to attract people that have the same interest as you.

Additionally, Google now has Google+ and Google hangouts. These are growing and emerging into two of the major social networking platforms. You can join the communities and

Google hangouts with others that are in the same business as you and have similar interests as well. It can also be a great tool for group video conferencing, masterminding, and brainstorming with your fellow investors or partners. To learn more about Google hangouts, visit their website at www.google.com/+/learnmore/hangouts

There are a many other social networking platforms out there. However, I don't want you to get lost in the social media world right now. I **DO** want you to create an account and focus on joining different real estate investors groups on LinkedIn, Facebook, and Google+. Remember to be active, engaged in the discussions, connect with people and create lasting mutually beneficial relationships.

Check out my website to receive more in-depth training on how to use social media to build relationships, grow your business, and generate leads.

Ok, the reason why I spent so much time on networking on and offline is because I want you to be successful in everything, not just real estate, and THE KEY TO YOUR SUCCESS LIES IN THE QUALITY OF RELATIONSHIPS YOU CREATE! Forming key relationships will make all the difference to the growth, development and profitability of your business. There is a reason why people say, "it's not what you know, it's WHO you know" but most importantly "it's not who you know, it's WHO KNOWS YOU"!

There is an even more powerful quote that says, "**Your network equals your net worth**". As someone who is just starting out brand new and doesn't know anyone in this industry, networking and building key relationships is not something you SHOULD do. It's something you **MUST** DO!

So now that you understand how crucial it is for to you to BUILD MEANINGFUL RELATIONSHIPS with the right people, you have to approach this the right way. This CANNOT be done by just simply attending meetings to pass out and collect business cards. Let's keep it real. How many business cards have you collected throughout the years? Now, how many of those people do you actually remember? Here's an even better question, where are most of those business cards at right now? There is nothing memorable about handing somebody a plain business card, everyone does it and no one keeps them.

I have a system that I call D.I.M.S. It means Be Different, Be Interested (in them), Be Memorable, and Be Selfless. Whenever and wherever you are networking, just remember D.I.M.S. This is how you can stand out from your competition and become memorable.

Now, am I telling you NOT to order business cards for yourself? Absolutely Not! You need them. Business cards do come in handy. When I send out letters to property owners to inquire about properties that I come across while I'm out driving around, I insert my business card in the envelope along with the letter. By the way, I always keep stamps, envelopes and a notebook in my car at all times, and you should too, so that when you come across a property that could be a potential deal, you can send out a letter immediately.

But, when you attend networking events, instead of focusing on randomly passing out your business cards to everyone, make it a habit of collecting the cards of the people you connect with so you can follow up with them later. When you meet people, get to know them. Get to know what they do and what their area of focus is. Pay close attention to what they may need so that you can identify the ways you can be a good resource to that person. Perhaps there are ways that you can personally help them or better yet, after you get to know what they do you can potentially send a few leads and referrals their way.

The only way you can help others is by being *interested in* **THEM**. You cannot connect with people by only focusing on yourself. Keep this in mind when you attend these meetings. Quality is more important than quantity. You do not need to meet everyone in the room only to be forgotten after the meeting is done. You can make 3 solid connections that you end up doing numerous deals with that can literally change your life and your business.

Almost a decade ago I bought my first set of 10 properties from a gentleman that I met at one of our local investors meetings. At that time there were over 100 people attending these meetings. The same guy also introduced me to other investors who I ended up buying more properties from using no money down strategies, not to mention the fact that I could call him for advice whenever I ran into issues on other deals I was working on. Again, focus on quality and not quantity. **Create relationships that pay.**

So remember, **D.I.M.S.** Be **Different**, Be **Interested** (in them), Be **Memorable**, and Be **Selfless**. And when you order your business cards make sure it's different, interesting, and it stands out. Create a card that somebody actually wants to keep. Your main goal is to be the one on the forefront of everyone's mind when they are looking to buy, sell or make a referral about a property. Be memorable and make sure your marketing materials help you remain memorable.

You can get a Free set of business cards at www.vistaprint.com. You can find a good graphic designer to design a very nice layout for your business cards for as little as $5bucks on www.Fiverr.com. Fiverr is a website where you can get many, many different types of services for as low as $5.00. I know people love to say, "You get what you pay for," but Fiverr is truly a website where you can get good professional work very cheap that would otherwise cost you tons of money elsewhere.

You can even find someone on there to set up your website for you. I have used people on there to do graphics work for me, edit videos, and even to create promo videos. In fact someone on fiverr designed the cover of this book that you are reading. I have used the same freelancer to design a couple of pages on my website, not the entire site, but a few of the graphics were done by her for $5bucks. You can't beat that. I love fiverr.com.

The key to finding the best freelancers on fiverr is to check out their reviews and ratings by customers who have used them. Also many of the sellers post examples of jobs (called "gigs") they have created for other customers on their order page. Check them out. When you place your order you have to be extremely specific about what you want. You can never be too specific because they will give you exactly what you ask for. Trust me. I had to learn this the hard way. But look on the bright side: worst case scenario, if your order gets screwed up, you will have only lost out on $5, so it's not the end of the world. And if you DO run into any issues with a seller/freelancer, you can dispute it through fiverr's internal system. So there aren't many downsides to this. Check them out. I think you will be pleasantly surprised at the type of things you can get done for $5.

In summary, networking and building key relationships is vital to your success in this business for many reasons. In addition to obtaining valuable education, developing meaningful contacts, creating beneficial partnerships, and introductions to other professionals, you can also generate many referrals and leads from other investors. Yes, other people that are actively buying and selling real estate can feed you leads as well. I will discuss this later.

Working With Real Estate Agents

Work with investor-friendly real estate agents.

You will need real estate agents on your team, specifically "investor-friendly" real estate agents. Investor-friendly real estate agent simply means that the agent has experience working with real estate investors and may perhaps be investors themselves.

I am personally an example of this. I am both a real estate agent and an investor. Investor-friendly agents are very aggressive and know how to get the best deals. Unlike most OTHER real estate agents, they understand exactly how investors work and make their money. They are not afraid to make what some would consider the "odd" and "low-ball" offers and they don't freak out when they hear the word "creative" (as in Creative Real Estate Investing), or act like it's a dirty word. A good agent can become one of your best sources for both buyer and property leads.

When you attend the real estate investors (REIA) meetings, be sure to have the other investors refer you to a few good investor friendly agents. When you are driving around looking for properties to invest in, look out for the realtor and agent signs. See who has many listings in the area. Contact them and introduce yourself. Tell them what your buying criteria are. Let them know the type of properties and deals you are looking for. Most importantly, tell them that you are a cash buyer, you have access to private funds and you can close quickly. Real estate agents love cash buyers because it means a fast closing, less headaches, and they will get paid fast.

When your agent brings you a great deal that fits your buying criteria, you have to be ready to take action on it. When you commit to a deal, make sure you follow through on that commitment, because besides the seller, real estate agents work for commission. They don't get paid until the deal closes. You want them to feel confident in knowing that you are a SERIOUS buyer and when they do bring you a good deal, you will act on it right away. You need to be able to follow through and CLOSE that deal, unless there is a valid reason (NOT a fault of your own) that you cannot.

Real estate agents have access to several buyers, but you want to be on favorable terms with the agents so they can call you, and ONLY you, when they come across a good deal. In order to get an agent to do that, you are going to have to prove yourself. They need to trust you, and **the best way to build that trust is to follow through on your commitments**.

Keep in mind that there are many other services that real estate agents can offer you that won't cost you any money up-front. Realtors typically have access to the Multiple Listing Service (MLS). Besides using the MLS to search for properties, they can also use it to do comparable searches and analysis, research market data, find recent cash buyers, and many other services that will benefit you as an investor. Start building relationships with real estate agents in the areas where you are going to investing in because they can be a great resource for you.

Working With Mortgage Brokers

Mortgage brokers are also a potential lead source for you.

Mortgage brokers and loan officers are also real estate professionals that you can build a mutual beneficial relationship with. There are multiple ways in which mortgage brokers can be of service to you, but for now I'm only going to focus on what's relevant to the lessons I cover in this book.

People apply for mortgages with loan officers and mortgage brokers whenever they need a loan to buy properties, refinance their properties, or obtain home equity lines of credit. The property (or collateral) could be an investment property, a 2nd home, or an owner occupied property.

There are several reasons why a person would want to refinance their home or take out an equity line of credit. Some people are looking for a lower interest rate to lower their monthly payments. Others are looking to go from an adjustable-rate mortgage over into a fixed-interest-rate mortgage. And then there are others who are looking to pull some of the equity out of the property to get their hands on some cash, and they may do this for any number of reasons. It could be that they are in a financial bind, or they could be struggling with some form of hardship and need the money to take care of their problems. Regardless of the need, many homeowners normally contact a mortgage broker or loan officer to apply for a cash-out refinance or a home equity line of credit to get the cash they need.

While mortgage brokers work hard to get as many loans as possible approved, there are a handful of people that cannot qualify. There could be numerous reasons for this. It could be because of poor credit score and credit history, insufficient income, or their debt-to-income ratios may be too high. Sometimes the property itself could be the problem and the reason why the loan cannot be approved. It may not appraise for the value that's needed to support the loan amount, or there could be physical problems reported in the property inspection report, which raises concern with the lender. If a lender feels that it is too risky to make a loan to an applicant they will most likely deny that loan.

When someone desperately needs cash and have exercised every option available to them, including refinancing their home to get that cash and still cannot get the money they need, that is a major problem for them. That "problem" that the homeowner now has, can become a potential investment opportunity for you.

Even if this person did not want to sell their house before, they would be much more open to selling now if their situation is so grave that the cash they need becomes more important than keeping their property. This is what we, in the real estate industry, call a "motivated seller". This is an opportunity for you to actually HELP this person. If you structure the deal right, you can create a win/win situation, where you help them get the cash they need to free themselves of whatever hardships they're going through while you buy a property at a deep discount that you can either wholesale/flip to another investor without investing any money into it, or you can close on the property yourself. If you choose you can then renovate the property and sell it retail or keep it as a rental so you can collect some monthly cash flow.

The point is that loan officers and mortgage brokers come across "dead files" all the time. A "dead file" simply means that the customer/borrower was "denied" or "not approved" for the loan and they cannot help them any further.

So start building relationships with mortgage brokers and loan officers. When you speak with them, explain what you do, and how you can help applicants that are turned down for loans. You must understand that they cannot just hand over their clients' name and phone number to you, but when they have clients in desperate situations that you can potentially help; they can connect the two of you with the client's permission. In exchange, you can send them leads and referrals because your marketing efforts will generate calls from all types of buyers. You will find that many of them need the services of a mortgage broker or loan officer. You and your fellow investors will also need someone to pre-qualify your buyers for your retail deals. Those are potential leads you can send them as well. So you both can feed each other leads. There are other services that loan officers and mortgage brokers can provide for you as well, but I won't be covering them in this book.

What Is Wholesaling & Why Is It Right For You?

Wholesaling is the fastest and one of the most effective ways to make money in real estate.

Now, before I get deep into how you can find and close deals quickly through wholesaling, let's talk about what wholesaling is and what it can do for you.

When we use the term wholesaling, it just means that you are buying and selling properties at a significant amount below market value, which leaves enough equity in the deal for your end buyer (who is usually an investor) to make a profit if they want to fix up the property and sell at retail value. And if they want to hold onto that property, buying a deal at a wholesale price gives the investor instant equity.

Wholesale properties are normally considered "distressed properties" because they typically need some repair, and/or the sellers are in some form of "distressed situation". I will go over this shortly. As a wholesaler, you will place those properties under contract and assign (sell) that property to another investor. You are basically the "middle man". You do not need to have a real estate license to do this. You only need to have "interest" in the property, and the fact that you have that property under contract gives you that "interest".

The contract you use to secure these types of deals should be an "assignable contract". If prepared correctly, it gives you the right to assign the contract to another buyer. You do not have to own that property, or be a real estate agent in order to sell it. The contract is what gives you that right to assign your interest to someone else. You can do this for a fee, and that person ("assignee") will have to abide by the original terms you and the seller agreed to per the contract. So you are only the "middle man" in the deal. This is how you can buy, sell, and even rent real estate without ever owning it. Now, let's move on.

You can wholesale any type of property, and in a number of different situations.

For example, you can wholesale:

- Short sales

- Bank-owned properties

- Properties where the owner still has a balance left on the mortgage and is

- not facing foreclosure.

- Properties that are free and clear, meaning the owner does not owe any

- money on it at all.

- Properties that have tons of liens and judgments against them.

- "Pretty" properties that have been recently renovated or even newly built.

- Properties that need a minimal amount of cosmetic work.

- Properties that are run down or condemned and may need to be torn down.

- Small to large apartment complexes, commercial buildings, and shopping

- centers.

These are just some of the situations where a wholesale deal may work.

You can even wholesale your spouses if you want! Some of you might like to... Ok, I'm totally joking. LOL.

There is no limit to the types of properties you can wholesale but I'm only focusing on residential properties in this book.

For a beginner like you, that wants to get in this business with limited funds, wholesaling offers many benefits. It is one of the easiest strategies you can use to get deals done and make money quickly, since it requires very little to no out-of-pocket expense from you.

You can literally negotiate a great deal with a property owner and secure the terms of that deal with a contract, then turn around and assign that contract to an "end-buyer" for a fee. The "end-buyer" is simply another person who is interested in purchasing that same property from you. The end-buyer is the one who then brings the cash to the closing table and takes title (or ownership) of the property under their own name or their business name. Once the funds to pay for that property (aka "funds to close") clear the bank, the title company will then cut you a check for whatever you sold (assigned) that contract for, which could range from hundreds of dollars to several thousand dollars.

The amount of money you make on each transaction depends on how good of a deal you can negotiate, first with the property owner and 2nd with your end-buyer. An average wholesaling fee could range from $2,000 to $5,000, but you can easily make $10,000, $15,000, $20,000 or more on a wholesale deal. There is no such thing as a cap on how much money you can earn on each deal.

And the best thing about all of this is that when you are wholesaling properties that you get from private owners and non-financial institutions (such as partnerships or investment companies), you never have to take ownership of that property. The ownership is transferred directly from the property owner to your end-buyer in those types of transactions. You are simply selling (which I have referred to repeatedly as "assigning") your rights to the contract that you negotiated and executed with the property owner. It's that simple.

Now, when you are buying properties from banks and other financial institutions, the transactions are still simple, but with a slight difference because the rules and regulations have changed over the last few years. Now that most banks no longer allow the standard assignment of contracts, you have to do what we call a "double closing". This is where you close the property with the bank and take title to the property first, and once that transaction is complete, you can then close with your end-buyer. Just so you understand clearly, there are two separate transactions that happen when you do a double closing, but they both can be done back-to-back on the same day.

The most important and CRUCIAL part to being successful when doing these type of deals is making sure that you are working with a **title company that is "investor friendly" and experienced in handling these types of transactions**, especially since you're new to the process. The title company MUST record the deed on the first transaction between you and the bank (or in the case of a short sale, it would be the homeowner) first, before they can record the deed between you and your end-buyer.

Wholesaling and investing in bank-owned properties is just as easy to do as properties that are privately owned.

Many bank-owned properties are listed with real estate agents. The banks normally require or demand an earnest money deposit (EMD), at the time that they accept your offer. The amount they require could range from $500 to $5,000 or more. This depends on the property, the price, and the competition that you may be bidding against. Many times they receive multiple offers for the same properties. If you are in a competitive market, you may run into situations where there

49

are multiple offers or bids on the same properties quite often, especially if it's a great deal. In my area an average requested EMD is normally about $1,000.

When you are dealing with a private seller (non-banks or financial institutions) you can negotiate a far less EMD, as little $1, especially if there are no real estate agents involved. Real estate agents typically push for buyers to put up a larger earnest money deposit to protect their sellers from buyers backing out of the deal (often called "buyer's remorse"). However, when you are dealing directly with a seller and they trust you, most times they won't even ask you for an EMD. At least that has been my experience and the experience of other investors I know.

Just a quick note: It is normal for a buyer competing for the same property as you to offer the seller a higher EMD to increase their chances of getting their offer accepted. This often happens in cases where a property is listed with a real estate agent.

If you are dealing in a transaction where YOU have to put down an earnest money deposit, make sure that you have your title company, attorney, real estate broker or an escrow company handling that EMD. **Do not make your check out directly to the owner in case of any possible dispute that may come up**.

Remember this: when you are dealing with your END-BUYERS, make sure that THEY put up a **non-refundable** earnest money deposit. That amount can be whatever you determine, but the average in my market is $2,000. You want to make it non-refundable because this represents the seriousness of your buyer. It is less likely that they will back out of the deal if they stand to lose a few thousands of dollars. **This is why it is important for your end-buyer to do their homework BEFORE they place your property under contract and lock up the deal**. Once they lock that deal up, you are not able to market the property to other buyers. The up-front earnest money deposit lowers your risk of having your buyer walk away because of "buyer's remorse".

Find the people with cash, or access to cash, educate them and show them how to make a sizeable return on their money through real estate investing. They can become your buyer, partner, lender or all of the above!

In cases where you need up-front cash for an earnest money deposit, you need to BE RESOURCEFUL. If you do not have the money required for the deposit, partner with someone that does and you can do one of two things:

When the deal closes, **a)** You can either split the profit with them 50/50, or **b)** You can offer them a return on the money they lend you. If you stand to earn $5,000 or more on a wholesale deal, and you need to borrow $1,000 from someone else to make that happen, offer to double their money. You can pay them back $2,000 (their original $1,000 + $1,000) for lending you the money. The person will probably assess the situation to see if the return you offer them is worth the risk. Often, you may be able to move the deal and pay them back within 2 to 3 weeks. That's one or two week's pay for most people. Borrow from two different people if you have to. **Just get out of your shell and get the money that you need together to make the deal happen**.

In summary, the most important factor in a wholesale deal is the fact that you as the wholesaler are able to get that property at a huge discount below its current market value, which enables you to turn around and resell that property at a discount to your end-buyer as well. Wholesale properties are normally good deals, and this why you are able to sell these properties quickly to cash buyers.

The Reason You're Able To Buy These Properties Cheap

Go where the hardships are, and there you will find your motivated seller.

As I mentioned before, the reason you are able to get these wholesale properties at such a huge discount is because there are normally special circumstances surrounding that property and/or the owner. This is why many wholesale properties need repair. However, the property itself is not always the issue. You will come across properties that are in perfect move-in condition that you can purchase at wholesale prices. Most times the property owners have some type of problem that is forcing them to sell. You have to learn how to identify those situations, because wherever you find hardships, you may find a motivated seller that NEEDS YOU to deliver them from a problem property.

Here are a few situations that may cause property owners to sell at a significant discount:

Some owners inherit properties that they do not want; they would rather have the cash and move on. Sometimes there are multiple heirs that inherit a property that they would rather sell and split the proceeds amongst them.

People who go through divorces tend to liquidate their assets to sever anything that keeps them bound within the EX-relationship. Sometimes, a seller may be facing bankruptcy, an unexpected tragedy, or experiencing health problems. Other times, people have to move in order to be with loved ones, and cannot afford two house payments and/or the cost to maintain 2 properties at the same time. Job relocation, or worse, the loss of a job, could be a factor as well.

Some people have rental properties and absolutely HATE the hassles that come with being a landlord. So they try to rid themselves of the agony and headache they may be experiencing with that role. And then, there are people who have large amounts of liens and judgments and they are forced to sell that property in order to pay off those debts.

Some property owners make the mistake of overestimating the amount of money it would take to repair their property and bring it back up to code and livable condition, while other sellers just want to liquidate their investments so that they can either retire or make other investments. I have even run across people who simply wanted a fresh start, and were not concerned about getting maximum dollars for their property. They actually admitted that!

There are also older sellers that want to downsize because they no longer want the trouble of maintaining a bigger house. When the kids get older and move out, they want a smaller, more intimate, and more manageable living space. I have also heard from a few owners that have joked and said that they want their houseguests to go home. No guest room = no more guest! It solves the problem, doesn't it? I actually find that funny. And believe it or not, there are some people whom you will meet, that will only want to sell their property to YOU and no one else, because they really like YOU. This means that they'll work out the most favorable terms for you so you will buy the property. I've been blessed to experience this.

There are endless situations that surround real estate deals, and these "sticky situations" are the reasons why we are able to buy properties at the low prices that we do.

The longer you are in this business, the more you will come across very different and unique situations. The fact is, I can probably write another ENTIRE book on the reasons why sellers sell their properties at huge discounts. Only very few of them choose to, but most of them realize that they HAVE to. This is why you need to learn how to be resourceful and learn to think creatively because that's what it takes to get many (if not most) of these deals done successfully.

Short sales, pre-foreclosures, foreclosures, and bank-owned properties offer a big opportunity for you to buy properties at huge discounts as well.

The point that I want you to understand here is this:

Because MOST of the reasons why sellers would agree to sell their properties so cheap are surrounded by some form of hardship, they are usually VERY motivated to get rid of that property quickly. Also, they want to do this with as little hassle as possible. They are even MORE motivated by the thought of cold, hard cash in their hands so they will often accept a "low-ball" offer just to get rid of their problems.

They usually want and need their cash soon, so a quick closing is even more of an incentive for them to lower their price. Keep this very valuable point in the forefront of your mind when you are looking for and negotiating your deals. GO WHERE THE PROBLEMS ARE.

Don't just randomly look for properties. Look for sellers with these types of "sticky situations". Go where the hardships are, and there you will find your motivated seller. This is the reason why you need to market your wholesale properties specifically to cash buyers. You need to be able to close these deals quickly, deliver on your promises, and help your sellers solve their problems, because YOU ARE A PROBLEM SOLVER.

Who Can You Sell Your Properties To

Many wholesale properties are not able to qualify for traditional loans because of their poor condition. This will be the case with most of the wholesale properties you will encounter. Therefore, those properties have to be sold to buyers who can pay with either cash or loans obtained from private or hard money lenders.

You will attract all types of buyers from your marketing efforts. Not all your buyers will be real estate investors. For example, you will attract a handful of cash buyers who are simply looking for a place to live. You will also find buyers who are looking for one or two investment properties to rent out so they can create some extra cash flow. And then there's MY favorite, buyers who are looking to buy several properties each month.

All of them matter to you and your business. However, you especially want to build relationships with the investors who will continuously buy multiple properties. Wouldn't it be great to sell your properties to them over and over again? Having these buyers at your immediate access will save you a lot of time and help you make a ton of money. They will help you save time because you can literally have your properties sold within minutes, with just a phone call. Buyers like these will close the deal as soon as your title company is ready, which could be as soon as 24 hours from the time they sign the contract. Of course, that will depend on the complexity of the deal and the workload of the title agent.

I cannot stress enough HOW IMPORTANT it is for you to build your network and put the right folks around you. This also applies to your buyers and investors who will continuously buy properties from you. These relationships that you build will HIGHLY increase your chances of making money in this business!

Keep reading, because there are a few more relationships that you need to form when you get started in this business with no cash. I will also go over how you will find the properties that you are going to sell, how you will market them, and the types of investors that you will sell these properties to, so stay focused and keep reading.

Create Relationships That Pay

ONE-SIDED RELATIONSHIPS DO NOT LAST and do not pay! You must bring your fair share of value to the table as well.

Now, I know that you are starting with a blank slate. At this moment, you most likely don't have any properties to sell, buyers to buy them, and you may not have any cash (I bet SOME of you do!). DON'T WORRY! Many people got started in real estate the SAME WAY, "broker than broke" and it's no joke. I know your pain; I've been there. So, that's perfectly fine.

Since I have already touched on the importance of networking, let's take things a bit further. You are starting with nothing and you want to get paid, so you need to create relationships that pay. It's now time to start forming the key relationships and partnerships with the right people that will make up for the things that you don't have. This is not a one-sided relationship; you will have to bring some value to the table. I'm going to teach you exactly how to do that and how to create "win/win relationships" and partnerships that can get you paid.

If you remember from the list of things you need to get started, I mentioned that you need properties that you can market and sell. However, if you are starting with limited funds and resources, I can see how you may think that this is going to be a difficult task to get done. Don't worry, because "difficult" does not mean "impossible". In fact, it's quite simple. Keep reading because later on I'm going to show you exactly what you need to do to get over this challenge.

Co-Wholesaling: Your Fast Track To Cashing In

Form partnerships that pay. That is the main key to unlocking your success in this business.

If you are serious about getting a deal done right away, you need to find out which wholesalers are actively doing business in your area. Real estate wholesalers are constantly buying and selling properties so they will normally have an inventory of properties available for sale.

To get started, you need properties to market and sell. And since wholesalers have properties in their inventory, this gives you the opportunity to make an arrangement with the wholesalers to market their properties and bring a buyer to the table. This is often referred to as "Co-Wholesaling". You can create a Joint-Venture partnership with them, find buyers to close on the deals, and split the profits.

Another way that you can form partnerships with other wholesalers is by having them bring you BUYERS for your deals. The experienced wholesalers normally have a list of buyers always ready to buy. If you can provide the properties that you have under contract, you can simply JV (joint venture) with them in this case as well. They can market the property, sell it to one of their buyers and the two of you can split the profits.

Everyone structure their deals differently, so it is important to discuss the details of each deal to make sure the both of you are on the same page about the deal and about your profit split.

There will be times when a wholesaler will buy your properties outright. At that point, they can do whatever they choose to do with the property, but chances are they will end up selling it to one of their buyers. Some wholesalers have their own rental portfolio and will occasionally rehab properties. One of the reasons why they may decide to buy a property outright from you is because they may see an opportunity to make more money on the deal, or they may see potential in that property and want to add it to their own investment portfolio. As long as you made your money, do not concern yourself with what someone ELSE chooses to do with THEIR property. And remember that if someone buys a property from you, and ends up selling it at a higher price where they make more money than you, that shouldn't be your concern either. Take your profit and move on to the next deal. After all, you are the one who originally set the price of the deal. Don't be greedy!

Don't count other people's dollars; only worry about your own. That's one of my pet peeves. They worked hard to generate the resources that they have. Just like you are working hard to develop your own resources. When it's your turn to skyrocket, the last thing you want is someone telling you how much you should be or shouldn't be making.

While you are marketing other wholesalers' properties and working on building your contact list of cash buyers, you can simultaneously work on building your own inventory of properties. The bottom line is you need to find good deals that you can sell. Go out and locate these deals, start making offers, negotiate a good price, get them under contract, then turn around and sell them to either a cash buyer or a buyer who has access to private money or "hard money" loans.

In the following sections I'm going to teach you how to find buyers and investors to sell your deals to. I will tell you what information you need to gather from your buyers so you can send them the best deals. I will also teach you how and where to find wholesalers to partner with. And after that, we'll go over different strategies you can use to find deals online and offline. You will learn about evaluating your deals and negotiating a great deal with your sellers. Keep reading.

SandyC Suggest: **CYA. Tips and WARNING:** One thing you need to be careful of when it comes to co-wholesaling and marketing properties for resale that you do not own is being accused of providing real estate brokerage services and dealing in real estate transactions without a real estate license. You want to be careful not to violate your state licensing laws.

Each state has their own specific rules and regulations in place, which describe or define which real estate "activities" require a state license or not. As a quick disclaimer, I would encourage you to look up the state licensing codes for where you will do your transactions or seek the advice of a real estate attorney because I am not an attorney. So, here is a quick and simple breakdown regarding this matter.

First of all you should know that these laws are mainly set in place to protect the public from predators and also to keep all parties fair and honest, especially in cases when a licensed individual is acting on the behalf of buyers and sellers for some sort of compensation.

So, before you can sell or market any property for resale you must have "an interest" in that property. When you start getting your own properties under contract, in those cases you will have a signed purchase and sales agreement directly between you and your seller. That contract gives you "an interest" in that property. As I discussed in previous sections, this contract that you have to buy that property is what then gives you the right to "sell and/or assign" your interest in the property to another without a real estate license. **So in this situation, you are acting on "your own" behalf and not on behalf of somebody else for a fee.**

What about when another wholesaler has the property under contract and you want to market that property to sell to your buyer? You need to have an "equitable interest" in that deal as well so you can legally market and sell it. Otherwise you would be performing real estate brokerage services for another person for a fee, which could potentially result in you facing some serious issues and fines if you do not have a real estate license.

When you are in a JV or co-wholesaling scenario, you have to secure your interest in that deal/property with either an assignment contract, an option contract, or even a signed purchase and sales agreement. The contracts you use will depend on the specifics of each deal. Either way, these documents gives you a contractual interest and right to market, sell and/or assign your interest to that property to your end-buyer and collect your profit at closing.

Identify Your Buyers & Know Their Strategy

Every investor has their own strategy and buying criteria. Find out what types of deals your investors are looking for secure those types of deals then sell the deal to them... Over and over again.

Each of your buyers will have their own investing strategy. They also have different levels of risk tolerance. As a wholesaler, you will come across different types of buyers and each have their own preferences or property types, particular neighborhoods, price range, the amount of profit they want to make, and the return they want on their investment (ROI). Some investors are purely looking for cash-flow and are not at all interested in fixing or flipping. Other investors are not interested in fixing anything, period. They only want the "turnkey" properties. Then, there are those investors who do not want to have anything to do with tenants. They don't want to be landlords or property managers even when they know they can hire a property manager to do the work for them and deal with their tenants.

Never assume what your buyers are thinking. If you do, you could be in for a big shock and watch what you thought was a sure deal slip right through your fingers.

Your job is to find out what your buyer's goals are.

Learn to ask them the right questions. This is the only way you will be able to help people solve their problems. You will never come up with the right solution to a problem by using the wrong formula. Find out what's important to your buyers as it relates to the transaction in addition to what resources they have and need to make a successful transaction.

You need to know if they are a cash buyer or using some sort of financing. You need to know this up-front, because most of your wholesale deals can only be sold to cash buyers or buyers using funds from a private sources or hard money lender. Ask them what types of properties are they interested in or have bought before. It could be single-family dwellings, multi-family dwellings such as duplexes, triplexes, or more. You need to know if they are looking for properties that they can buy, fix and flip to a retail buyer, a turnkey property for other investors, or to buy, fix and rent for the longer-term.

If they are buy and hold investors, find out what types of tenants will they be renting to, Section 8 tenants or traditional tenants. Ask them if are interested in block construction or if they buy wood frame or even manufactured homes as well. You also need to know which neighborhoods they prefer to invest in, and the price range. How many bedrooms and bathrooms do these properties have to be? If the property does not have the amount of bedrooms or bathrooms they want, but the floor plan would make it easy to add an extra bedroom and/or bathroom, would they still be interested if everything else meets their criteria? Find out how extensive a rehab/renovation they are willing to do. And most importantly, find out when they will be ready to buy! Some investors are buying often and always ready to grab a great deal, but the first time you talk to them, you need to ask so you will know.

SandyC Suggest: Practice listening. Do this with everyone; buyers, sellers, lenders, and your potential partners. Even practice this in your personal life. People will tell you a lot without saying much. Even when you're not talking about deals, just listen, because through listening you will hear clues as to what people's "real motives" are. Through listening, you can find out WHAT they really want and WHY. Those "emotional checkpoints" really matter.

In this business of buying and selling houses, **you need buyers who CAN CLOSE QUICKLY**. So that means that your end-buyers need to have cash on hand or have access to cash to be able to move fast on the great deals you will provide to them. One of the reasons why you will be able to convince sellers to accept a low-ball offer for their property is your ability to close immediately.

Since private lenders and hard money lenders have the ability to provide the funding necessary for your buyers to close transactions quickly, it is perfectly fine for your buyers to get their financing from them (if that is what it will take to make the deal happen). The important thing is they are able to close QUICKLY!

Most private and/or hard money lenders are able to process a loan and fund a real estate transaction within anywhere from 24 hours to a couple of weeks. If you are working a deal with no complications, it should NEVER take more than 3 weeks to get a deal funded. If it does, I would suggest that you look into the situation and have a backup buyer ready. Either way, you have to stay on top of what's going on with your deal, your buyer, and their funding source, especially if you haven't worked with them before.

This is the reason why it is important for you to have hard money lenders on your team. Some of your buyers will rely on you to direct them to a hard money lender that can help them fund the deals they will buy from you. If you are selling a property for $50,000 and your buyer is highly interested in that property but only has $25,000, you can direct them to one of your hard money lenders that can do that deal for them and loan them the remaining $25,000. This is money in your pocket. **If you want to learn more about finding and working with hard money lenders get my book "Hard Money Success Formula: The 18 Critical Must Ask Questions For Hard Money Lenders That Will Guarantee Funds For Your Real Estate Deals Every Single Time."**

While I'm on the topic of lending, you should know that while many of your deals can be closed using your buyer's funds, you are going to come across deals where you will have to come to the table with your own funds in order to make the deal happen. As in the case of double closings, you may have to fund the first closing, which is often referred to as the "A-B closing" before you can close with your end-buyer on the "B-C closing".

Let's say for example that you are closing on a bank-owned property. On the "A-B transaction", the "A" is your seller (in this case it is the bank that you are purchasing that property from) and the "B" is the buyer (you). On the 2nd transaction, the "B-C closing", the "B" is the seller (you) and "C" is your end-buyer, the person or company that you are selling the property to.

There are several ways that you can fund the "A-B transaction". One option is to use your end-buyer's funds, but let's not focus on that for THIS scenario. Another option would be to fund it yourself, but we will skip that option as well in THIS scenario, because we are assuming that you do not have the necessary cash to close. A third option is to find a partner with enough cash to fund your "A-B transaction", and you can split the profits on the deal, or give them the return they would be comfortable with in order to lend you the money.

You can also find a private lender that will lend you the money to close.

If you are out of all those options, there is something called "transactional lending" that you can count use. This involves lenders that will give you a short-term loan to close on deals such as this. They normally charge a flat processing fee plus a percentage of the amount of the loan and they collect this fee at closing. The charges vary from lender to lender.

To get a "transactional" loan, all they require is that you have a solid end-buyer in place. They will not check your credit or verify your income or any of those traditional qualifications that happen with other real estate loans. You will have to provide the contracts from the A-B and the B-C transactions and prove that your end-buyer has the money to close on the deal. In addition, you may need to prove that their earnest money has been deposited. They normally require that both transactions take place at same title company or attorney's office simultaneously, plus they will require some additional documents from your closing agent as well.

When you contact the transactional lender, you can get a list of their requirements and their fees, so that you can be prepared in advance. A transactional lender can fund the deal for you, but it will cost you. However, that money will be collected at closing and deducted from your proceeds, so it is not coming out of YOUR pocket. Again, use your network to get referrals for these lenders and take advantage of the power of Google in addition to my website.

Since the majority of your buyers will be landlords ("Buy & Hold" investors) and rehabbers ("Fix & Flip" buyers), let's quickly go over that.

Buy & Hold Buyers

Buy & Hold Investors buy properties for monthly cash flow (passive income), for long-term capital gain, and tax shelter.

Some of your buyers are what we call "buy and hold" investors. This means that when they buy these properties, they hold on to them over a long period of time to create passive income, for capital gains and even for the tax shelter.

Some of these investors buy properties to build their investment portfolio to a certain point where they can sell a portfolio of cash-flowing properties for a huge lump sum of cash. I have seen many investors sell their real estate portfolio, take their profit and either retire or invest into bigger projects such as commercial properties, apartment complexes, or land development projects.

Buy & hold buyers may rehab properties as well. Many of them will buy a discounted property that needs to be repaired before they can rent it out. Remember that buying properties that are distressed, gives them the opportunity to purchase the property below market value, thus giving them instant equity in the deal and increasing their profit. So although they intend to keep the property as a rental, they will rehab the property, make it livable and up to code, before they rent it out.

FIX & FLIP BUYERS AKA REHABBERS

Fix and Flip investors AKA Rehabbers will make up a large percentage of your end-buyers.

There are investors that will buy properties from you to fix it up and flip it at retail prices. They will be selling to buyers who are normally getting financing from major banks and financial institutions. Rehabbers have to buy properties at a discounted price, because they have many expenses to cover before they can even sell the property and make a profit on the deal.

They have to take into consideration the cost to cover all repairs and renovation. They also have "holding costs", which consist of utilities, maintenance, and "financing costs" (such as monthly interest payments to the lender that funded the deal). In addition, a rehabber also may have "acquisition costs" like closing fees and upfront financing fees. When they resell the property, they may have to pay closing costs (now as the seller), marketing costs, and real estate commission if they use a real estate agent to help them list and sell the property.

Your "fix and flip" buyers not only need to have a good "spread" on a deal, they also need to move their property as quickly as possible because the longer they hold on to that property, the smaller their profit gets.

HERE ARE A FEW SCENARIOS THAT COULD EXTEND THE SCHEDULE TO COMPLETE A REHAB PROJECT:

For a minor to moderate rehab, the process could take up to 90 days from the time they purchase the property to the time they resell the property. However depending on the extent of the rehab, challenges they may encounter, and if a permit is necessary, it could take a rehabber up to 6 months from the time they buy the property to the time they sell it to an end-buyer.

Some hard money lenders release funds for repair in phases. They either come out to the property themselves (if you are dealing with a smaller hard money lender), or they will send a property inspector out to the property to verify all of the work done. They will also check to see if the city inspector has signed off on the work before they release the money for the next phase. If a permit is required, that may take time as well. The amount of time it takes for a permit to get approved depends on their local building department and the type of permit needed.

When the rehab is complete, if your investor/rehabber is selling to an end-buyer who needs to get financed (most likely that is the case with retail buyers), they have to wait anywhere from 20 days to 45 days for the buyer's financing to close. This is because that retail buyer has to go through an underwriting process by the bank or financial institution.

The underwriting process requires lots of paperwork from that borrower, in addition to an appraisal (somtimes 2). They also generally require several different types of property inspections, such as termite, roof, and even sometimes structural, depending on the property and the transaction. After an underwriter requests all of these documents, they verify everything, and then they have what they "quality control" look at the deal before they sign off on everything and give the borrower a "clear to close".

These days, lenders are more careful before they approve a loan, because they do not want another borrower that will default on that loan. Just as there can be a few "unpredictable situations" that pop up in the renovation phase, there can be "unpredictable situations" that can pop up in the financing stage as well. A smooth transaction may take anywhere from 20 to 30 days.

These are the reasons why your "fix and flip" buyers have to have a good spread in the deals you offer them, otherwise they will lose their money and you could lose a long term relationship with a potentially good buyer.

The bottom line here is that all buyers are not created equal. Knowing who your end-buyer is will definitely affect your negotiation tactics and the terms and price you agree to.

Let's move on to getting to know your market and pricing. For someone with no prior experience, this can be a big challenge for you. The good news is that there are a few steps you can take, in addition to any coaching, that will make this process easier for you. If you are going to be successful in this business, you have to learn how to recognize a good deal when you see one and knowing your market is a good place to start.

Get To Know Your Market

Every market is different. It is vital that you get to know the market where you will be handling your transactions. What works in Detroit, Michigan might not work in Houston, Texas.

You need to become familiar with the communities you are buying and selling your properties in, because your investors will want to know this information as well. So learn as much as you can about them.

Your buyers /investors typically will ask questions like:

- Is the neighborhood a blue collar or white collar neighborhood?

- Is it in a "war zone"?

- You should know if there is anything special about that neighborhood such as:

- Is it in a historical district?

- Is there new construction going on, or new businesses coming into the area?

- Is it close to shopping centers, schools, churches, and major highways?

The more information you can tell your investors about the neighborhood, the better. You should know up-front what the selling points are for that neighborhood and that will help you sell that property faster.

You should also know if the residents in the community are mainly homeowners or tenants. You can often tell a neighborhood that is mostly occupied by tenants or homeowners by looking at their yard/landscaping. On an average, homeowners are likely to keep their lawns neat and trimmed. They take better care of the property than tenants do. There are tenants that take great care of the properties as well, but you are most likely to see evidence of pride of ownership in a property occupied by the actual homeowner. This is not the rule 100% of the time but it is something to take notice of while you are investigating the communities to invest in.

Supply And Demand

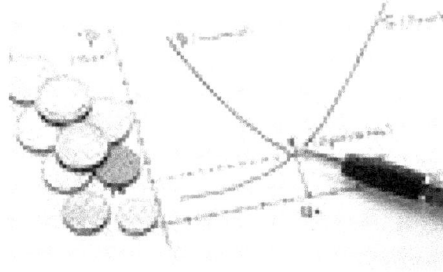

Both a buyers' market and a sellers' market present a set of opportunities and challenges. As a smart investor, you can capitalize in both market and help your buyers do the same.

In any real estate market, there are many variables that affect housing prices. First there is a matter of supply and demand. In real estate you will hear the terms "buyers' market" and "seller's market" thrown around a lot. Whether it's a buyers' market or sellers' market is a direct reflection of supply and demand.

In order to understand this, you have to look at the available "inventory" out there. You need to determine how many properties are available for sale (supply), and not only that, you also need to know how many people want to buy those properties available for sale, and do they have the means to buy those properties (demand). The bottom line is… can they afford it? In real estate, the ability to get cash or qualify for financing to pay for these properties plays a major role in demand. Also remember that demand is also affected by affordability, as well as availability, of employment and credit.

Let's Look At The Difference In Each Market:

In a sellers' market, the sellers are very happy because they get the better end of the deal. The houses sell quicker. Sellers normally get the price they want, and sometimes more. Housing prices tend to rise in a seller's market.

On the flip side, when you're in a buyers' market you will notice properties taking a longer time to sell, which makes a seller more open to a lower price and more flexible terms. As an investor you can use different strategies to profit in both markets.

Economic Variables

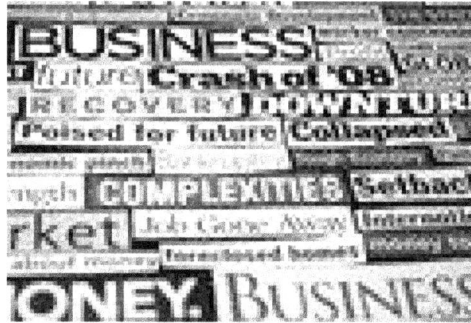

What are the major factors that affect housing prices in your area?

There are many factors that could either drive housing prices up or down in any area. There are variables that affect housing prices such as: social class, income level, availability of jobs, resources, credit (loans), in addition to other economic factors. You can research and obtain these types of datas through the U.S. Census Bureau. For example, if you take the town where you, you will see that there are submarkets within the main market. These sub-markets are segmented based on the different factors, which affect the outlook of that area. These factors affect the desirability of homeownership in that neighborhood, which in turn affects the housing prices in that community. It's like a ripple effect.

For example, lower-income neighborhoods typically have higher crime rates and are less desirable by homeowners (as well as many investors). In contrast, more affluent neighborhoods have lower crime rates, better-maintained properties, and generally have a much better school district.

Whether you are buying or selling, DO YOUR HOMEWORK and seek out the help of professionals if you have to.

The Quickest Way To Learn Your Market

You can learn tricks of the trade from other investors and wholesalers in just a matter of days that potentially can take you years to learn otherwise.

One of the quickest and easiest ways to get familiar with your market and the prices the investment properties are selling for is to locate all the active wholesalers and investors in your area. Get yourself on their "buyers lists" so you can receive all of the emails that they send out when they have new properties for sale. Most experienced wholesalers already have a list of potential buyers that they frequently send out emails to in order to notify them about properties they have for sale.

By getting on the wholesalers buyers list, you will get a good idea of what the price ranges are for wholesale properties in your area. The average prices could vary from neighborhood to neighborhood depending on the factors I previously discussed. Your job is to pay attention to those deals.

Get in your car, drive by those properties and check out the type of neighborhood they are in. Pay special attention to the physical condition of those properties. This will help you become familiar with how the properties are priced and how much a property should go for (on an average) based on its physical condition and location.

SandyC Suggest: Make sure you're not on just one person's list. Also, do not assume they've got their numbers right! Follow up after the property is sold. Find out how much the property sold for and at what terms, if you can. This information is public record so you don't have to worry about calling the wholesaler/investor to ask them this information unless you want to and have established that type of relationship with them. Either way, taking this extra step will confirm if that property was priced right.

Also, use the Internet to look for all the properties that are for sale in the area where you are doing your investing. Not only will you get a good understanding of what is available for sale in your area, but also you will begin to build a sense of how you should price your own deals. Always, Always, Always Do Your Own Due Diligence, but if you can get on the list of more than a few experienced wholesalers who already have a good understanding of the market this can become a quick way for you to learn. Practice caution, but use them as a guide.

Finding The Deals

There are plenty of properties out there for you to invest in. Learn how to spot the right deals and you will make a lot of money in this business.

There are a few things you need to keep in mind when you are looking for properties to buy and sell. Get to know your end-buyers and understand the type of investors they are, even down to their exit strategies. You can find these things out simply by asking them and by talking to them. They are usually more than happy to give you this information, because this helps you send them the best deals. You will avoid wasting your time OR theirs by sending them the wrong types of deals. As a wholesaler, you will have a wide range of buyers and you will be constantly adding new investors to your current list of buyers.

With that said, I want to point out that if you negotiate a good price for a property it really doesn't matter who your end-buyer is. You will be able to sell that property to just about anyone, even with a simple street sign. So when you run across a "steal" of a deal, grab it quickly, because if you market it right, you will be able to sell it just as quickly.

If you want to be able to sell your properties quickly, you need to consider the following questions when you are looking for deals to purchase:

1. What are the most desirable communities in your area?

2. What neighborhoods (or zip codes) are the landlords in your area buying in?

3. These areas require totally different strategies for you, the wholesaler. The first category could be the best or ideal place for you to buy single-family houses, rehab them and flip to retail buyers. Normally these are the areas where most of the residents are owner occupants as opposed to tenants. These are the areas where your rehabbers (Fix & Flippers) that buy properties to flip to retail buyers will be mostly interested buying in.

4. The second category describes areas that are not necessarily considered the best neighborhood for the typical homeowner or retail buyer, but are perfect for landlords who rent to Section 8 tenants. These are normally lower-income areas where the property values are on the lower end of the scale. A lot of transactions are taking place in those areas because these are the areas where many of your buy & hold investors are picking up their properties for dirt cheap, fixing them up, and renting them out to mainly Section 8 tenants, and making a killing in cash flow.

5. Which of the communities in your market sell the fastest?

For example, the competition can be fierce in some of the most desirable communities in your area, especially if the properties are priced right. The reason you should know about these communities is because for one, as a wholesaler this is a great selling point. If you are selling a property in that community to a rehabber/flipper and you can prove to them that they will be able to sell that house quick and collect their profit right away so they can move on to the next deal, they'll snatch that deal from you without blinking.

Secondly, most of the experienced investors in your area will already have a working knowledge about the popular communities in their market. If you have established a handful of serious cash investors, you want to send great deals from these areas to all of them. This can literally create a bidding war amongst them, which can drive up the price, thereby getting you a higher price than you initially set for it!

This is a win for you as well as for your investor, even if it's an investor that wants to hold onto that property. It is easier and quicker to secure tenants for a house that is located in a desirable community. To that landlord, this means they can start cash-flowing immediately. They won't have to worry about having an empty house sitting there for months, sucking money out of their pockets because of holding costs. Even in a situation where the investor owns the property free and clear without any mortgages, property owners will always have to pay costs to maintain that property in addition to property taxes and insurance. These bills never go away, whether you have a tenant or not. So the longer that property sits vacant, the more money it's costing that investor.

Also, an empty house is more vulnerable to vandalism by thieves, and sometimes it's just the kids in the neighborhood.

Regardless, damage that is caused by unwanted guests will create more work and more expense for the investor. So just understand that there are many benefits to buying properties in a desirable community, some of which I just mentioned.

So in summary, for you as the beginner investor and/or wholesaler, these are the things you need to keep in mind if you want to start generating cash quick for yourself. When you are out there scouting for deals, it is important for you to know the type of deals you will be able to move quickly.

Properties in desirable communities are easier to move (if they are not overpriced) because most people want them. Even investors that consistently buy properties in the less desirable neighborhoods will buy a great deal in the better area. There are many investors that actually start out investing in the more risky neighborhoods, and eventually shift to the better areas.

SandyC Suggest If the numbers and terms are right I will buy anywhere. And when I say "right" I mean dirt-cheap. This is what we call "a steal". Even if I don't intend to keep that property as a rental, I just know that I will able to move that property to an end-buyer easily and quickly if the deal is structured right and has lots of built-in equity. There is a buyer for everything when the price is right. In fact, when you have a great deal it is common to have multiple buyers interested. "When the price is right, the buyers fight." This is not rocket science and it is not top secret. Don't let anyone tell you any different.

As a wholesaler, most of your buyers will be investors. So when you come across a potential deal, it is crucial that you focus on the numbers and terms of the deal so you can work out the best scenarios you possibly can. You're not going to hit a home run every time, but being able to negotiate a great deal will help you sell that property faster even if you don't have a list of buyers. I will cover working your numbers later in this book.

The bottom line here is there must be LOTS of equity in the deal, and if the equity is not the best selling point, then the 'terms' of the deal better be. Everyone loves a great deal. Great deals are EASY to sell. The only way you can guarantee great deals to your end-buyers is if you negotiate a great deal with your sellers to begin with. Your investors are in this business to make a profit and so are you. In the business of buying and selling properties negotiate a steal and you will easily move that deal, even without a buyer's list.

Now, on to the good stuff.

There are many ways you can find properties to buy, both online and offline. I'll go over a few of the online methods first, and then we can discuss finding properties offline.

Finding Properties Online

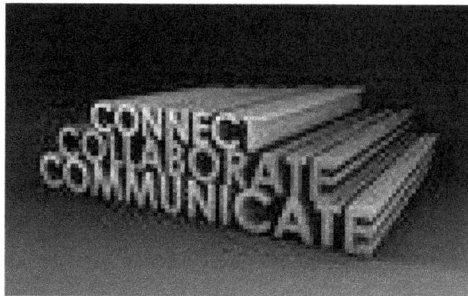

Always remember to connect with partners, share ideas, and keep the communication lines open. These factors are essential in maintaining relationships that pay.

Let's talk about how you are going to actually find deals. But before I get into the nitty gritty stuff, I want to remind you that you are now in the business of buying and selling houses so you need to let everyone you know about what you are doing. Chances are, if they know that you are in the business and they have a house to sell, they will contact you and give you the first opportunity to buy that property from them. And when they are ready to buy, you can potentially be the person that sells them their next property.

SandyC Suggest Leads are the lifeblood of your business. You have to Always Be Marketing (ABM) and be on the constant lookout for properties that you can buy and sell, and for buyers to sell your properties to.

There are many ways to sell a property and there are many strategies you can use to buy properties. I will not be able to cover all of these techniques in this book, but the saying "there's more than one way to skin a cat" applies to real estate investing as well. There are endless ways to invest and make money in real estate... However, I'm still looking for that person that actually skinned a cat and actually tracked it. Saying that out loud actually sounds creepy now. Ok moving on.

There are various websites and online resources you can use to find properties on the Internet. Be consistent with your search and be proactive.

Nowadays people count on the Internet for everything. I know I do and I'm betting you probably do too, or you are getting closer to being that way. Whether they are looking to buy or sell a property, both potential buyers and sellers start their journey online. So you have to take advantage of this.

There are many websites you can use to search for deals online. I will cover some of the basic details here, but at the end of the book I added a list of websites that you can use to search for all types of properties from FSBO (For Sale By Owner) properties to REO/ bank-owned properties websites. REO simply means Real Estate Owned. These are properties that the bank has taken back through foreclosure. Essentially, REO and bank-owned have the same meaning. I have personally used a handful of the websites I share with you at the end of this book to buy bank-owned properties online.

Craigslist

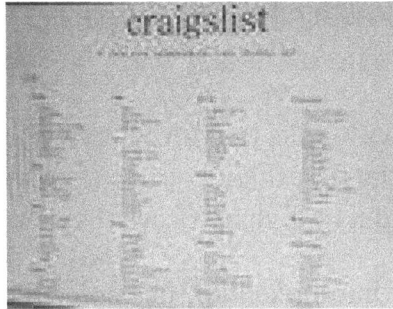

Craigslist is a great place to start your search. Millions of people use this website everyday to buy, sell and rent out real estate, but you must be consistent and proactive to get good results.

You can search for properties on online classified websites like Craigslist, www.craigslist.com and Backpage, www.backpage.com. You will have to make this a daily habit in order to find the good deals. Look in the real estate sections in your area or the area where you are buying. Search through the For Sale By Owner sections for deals. Some ads will have instructions telling how they want to be contacted. So you can either call or email them. A lot of your local wholesalers and investors constantly advertise on those websites as well, so this creates the perfect opportunity to get to know them. Capture their info, give them a call, introduce yourself, and ask about the deals they are working on.

You can follow the same rule for the other classified ads websites as you do with craigslist. I specifically wanted to focus on craigslist because it is a powerful tool you can use to generate leads and sell your properties if you stay consistent with use of it.

Here are a few ways to identify wholesalers online

When you are searching through the online ads for potential deals and you see the same name appear several times on different ads marketing different properties, chances are that person is a wholesaler.

If you see an ad with links that direct you to a website outside of craigslist and the first thing you see is an opt-in form asking for your email and name, chances are they are wholesalers.

If you see an ad that looks like the typical Postlet flyers with the pictures and details of a property, chances are that person is a wholesaler marketing that property.

Also, look at the entire ad and look for any mention of them having multiple properties for sale or looking for multiple properties to buy. All of these are clues that they could be wholesalers and/or flippers.

There are also other investors, like rehabbers and landlords that advertise their properties on those sites. Landlords advertise properties for rent and a rehabber may advertise a property they just finished renovating and are now selling. Look out for those as well because those people could potentially be your future sellers, buyers, and/or partners on deals.

SandyC Suggest: Here's a side note, since we are on the subject of finding wholesalers. One of the best ways to find wholesalers offline is by calling on the bandit signs that you see around your town while you are driving around. Those signs advertising other properties or looking for properties to buy are normally placed out there by other wholesalers. Call them up and find out how you two can work together.

Code Violation Properties

You can profit from properties with code liens and violations.

You can also find code violation properties online as well. Many counties now release their list of code violations properties on their city department websites. You can print out those lists and make contact with the owners, using the methods I discussed in this book. After you get in touch with the owner, get the payoff from the city to find out how much the past due fees are and find out what the violations are as well. Although each county is different, often times you can negotiate the fines down substantially and snag yourself a great deal.

There are other factors outside of the code enforcement lien that still affect the potential of a deal, such as an existing mortgage on the property, delinquent taxes and/or other liens and judgments. If the homeowner does not own the property free and clear, you need to find out how much they owe the lender on the property. You also need to know the current property value. You have to find out these details so you can structure the best deal possible.

Just as I'm wrapping this, a buddy of mine brought a deal to me that we ended up partnering on. This property had a code enforcement lien on it for $52,000. We negotiated the lien down to $1,500 with the county. In addition to the code enforcement lien, this property had back taxes. It was scheduled to be sold at the tax deed auction in just a matter of days. Long story short, I paid off the back taxes, which was $7,800 before it made it to the auction, got a quitclaim deed from the homeowner and we are selling the property without doing any repairs to it.

Rental Websites

There are several websites where you can find properties listed for rent. You can check out websites like Go Section8, http://www.gosection8.com, where landlords that are looking to rent to section 8 tenants post their properties. The other websites that I previously mentioned, such as craigslist, have tons of rental listings as well. Some of the landlords advertising on those sites may or may not be interested in selling, so call to inquire. You can also look up the owner and property info on the county's property appraiser's website to get the owner's mailing address so you can send them a letter. Keep in mind that these landlords are also potential buyers, as I said before, even if they are not interested in selling at the moment, they may want to buy more rentals to add to their portfolio. If they are looking for more properties to buy, you can sell to them also.

Finding Properties Offline

BANDIT SIGNS

Many investors and wholesalers use bandit signs to sell their properties because it works. Just be careful not to get fined by the "sign police".

You can also use bandit signs to attract sellers just like you use them to find buyers. You may have seen the "We Buy Houses" signs. That is one of the messages that some investors use to get sellers to call. The key here is to place these signs in the neighborhoods where you want to buy your properties from. First find out what the neighborhood and city code enforcement policies are before you place the signs out.

CAR WRAPS

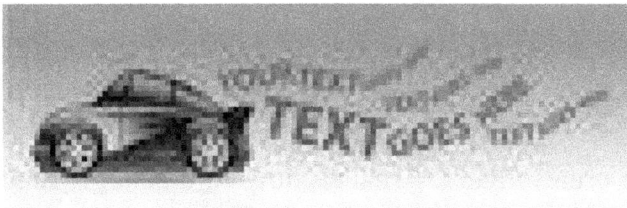

You can use your car as a mobile advertising billboard.

You can wrap your car with "I buy houses" or "We buy houses" message with your website and contact information so sellers can reach you. I don't personally do this, but if it can get you at least one extra deal then it could be worth it. You can be as creative as you want. I have seen some pretty creative ones with clever and catchy messages. The only thing I would say is if you are living in a deed-restricted community before you get the car wrap, just check to make sure that you're not violating any of the homeowners association's policies against commercial vehicles in the community.

FLYERS

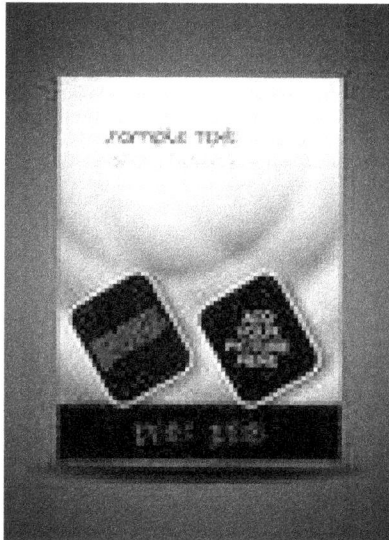

There are plenty of free templates online you can choose from to design an attractive flyer.

You can create flyers. I realize how "old school" that sounds but the fact of the matter is some "old school" methods still work. It is up to you if you want to test this to see if this could work for you. I have an investor friend that uses flyers to sell condos, and it works great for them. I have witnessed them putting out those flyers and selling units like hot cakes. They placed the flyers in high traffic areas, like shopping centers, and Laundromats within the neighborhood where they were selling those units. For them, the flyers worked perfect.

As I mentioned before, you can take those flyers to the REIA meetings with you. You can also distribute them at your church, local high traffic mom & pop businesses such as restaurants, beauty salons, day care centers, barbershops, etc. Just be creative with this strategy and think of high traffic places in that area and bring a few flyers there. Get permission if there is a "no solicitation" rule. Mom & pop businesses that you frequent will normally support you and allow you to place your flyers at their business. Place those flyers in areas where they will be easily seen and picked up by customers.

Flyers are not something I personally do because I don't have the patience for it. But if you're impatient like me, and you think flyers would benefit you, get someone else to distribute the flyers for you. You could find someone locally like a college student or look for someone on fiverr.com to distribute and even design it for you. If it lands you a sale, GREAT! If it gets you a few calls from interested people, that is awesome too, because those calls could turn out to be a potential sale for you. So work your magic.

REFERRALS AND WORD OF MOUTH

As soon as you make the decision to start buying and selling real estate, you have to let everyone around you know.

Everyone you know and everyone they know can be a source for referrals. You have to let people know what you do. Even your fellow investors can be a source of referrals for you. There are many reasons why an investor may determine whether they will do a deal or not and that can range from the type of neighborhood, to price range, to condition of the property, to available cash and resources, etc.

Sometimes they run across great deals that actually fit their investing model, but it's not in an area where they want to invest in. It could also be that the property is in a neighborhood they don't like or it could be too far out for them to get to regularly. There are even times when a deal fits an investor's model perfectly from every single detail down to the location, but their money is tied up in other deals and for whatever reason they are not willing to borrow money to do a new deal. In any of these cases, the investor will pass on the deal.

So it is very common for investors to run across properties that they are not interested in, for their own set of reasons. In situations where they don't want a particular property, they can forward those unwanted deals to you. Most of them won't ask for a dime for passing a lead to you. If you are actually able to close a deal that someone referred to you, it is a good idea to do something for them to show your appreciation. You can return the favor by giving them first "dibs" on your next deal that fits their criteria or even offer a gift card to their favorite restaurant. When people like you and trust you, they look out for you. This is why relationship building is so important.

DIRECT MAILING

Direct mailing is one of the most effective ways to target homeowners and generate seller leads. You must to be consistent with this type of marketing to get great results.

You can do a direct mail campaign where you can target a specific group of owners such as absentee owners, out of town owners, probate, pre-foreclosures, free and clear properties, bankruptcies, and even divorces, the list goes on and on. Since the purpose of this book is to show you how to earn cash so you can start building your capital right away, I would suggest that you stay away from targeting pre-foreclosures at this time.

You should know that Not all pre foreclosure properties are upside down. A property is considered to be "Upside down" when the homeowner owes more on the mortgage loan balance than the property's current market value. There are homeowners with plenty of equity in their home that simply cannot afford to continue making their mortgage payment and cannot refinance, thereby putting them at risk of losing their homes through foreclosure. However, in today's market, the majority of those properties are upside down and you will have to negotiate a short sale with the bank on those types of deals, which could take months.

You are looking for deals that can close quickly so you can start getting paid right away. Also, since there are so many homes that are upside down now, it's very easy to get those types of leads without having to spend so much marketing money to target them. Nowadays, you probably can find these types of leads in your own backyard.

Go to www.Cashin30days.com for alternative ways to monetize your short-sale and pre-foreclosure leads. If you are working with limited resources and cash, I would suggest you invest your money in advertising that will yield a quicker result for you because the goal is to start putting cash in your pocket right away. Once you start making money you can target other types of leads that fit your plan and budget but may take more time to close. If you are limited on cash and time, you want to focus your time only on activities that will generate income for you a.s.a.p.

Direct mail campaigns do require that you make a bit of an investment. You will need up-front money to buy a mailing list from a list broker such as www.listsource.com and www.melissadata.com in addition to buying stamps, envelopes, and paper (print or yellow notebooks). If you are going to hire someone to write the letters for you, you will need money to pay that person as well. You can also use services to send out printed postcards, in which cases you don't have to worry about, writing letters, stuffing and stamping envelopes.

When you are starting out, it is important to create a monthly budget to generate seller leads through mailing campaigns. If you are working with limited funds, you need to look at where you can cut back from your personal spending to get the money you need to invest in your business (that is if you are **truly serious** about changing your financial position). Don't say you don't have an extra $100 to $200 to invest in your business, if you are spending money on frivolous activities. Look where you can cut back so you can invest in your business.

However, if money IS really tight for you, you will have to target your marketing so that that it will yield you the greatest return. You may even have to do a lot of the leg work yourself initially, if you are starting off with low to no budget. So instead of buying a list from a list broker, you have a couple of alternative options. First, there are title companies that can pull any list for you. If you want to target absentee owners, free and clear properties, or any other list, title companies have access to a database with this information, especially the bigger or national title companies such as First American Title.

When I first got my real estate license, I remember an agent from these title companies would come to our office weekly to offer this service to us. The best thing is that they will generally do this for free. They just want your business when you find a deal out of their efforts. This is not a request that title companies get often from investors, so it is possible that not all title companies will understand how to help you with this matter in your area. The point is to make contacts with title agents, go visit them, and see how they can help you with your marketing.

Your second option is to go to your local Tax Assessor's office to pull the list of owners you are targeting and collect their mailing addresses. Many cities and counties now make this information accessible on the Internet. You will just have to invest the time to get this information yourself. After you generate your list and add them to your database, you can handwrite the mailing addresses on the envelope yourself and either send out "yellow letters", typed letters, or postcards to these homeowners every month. I know that it's 2013 and we're living in a new age of technology, but handwritten envelopes and letters normally get a higher rate of response. However, you can test both to see what works best for you.

You should target a list that fits your investing style in the beginning. For example, targeting absentee owners and free and clear properties can be very effective. An absentee owner simply means that the owner of the property lives somewhere else and not at that property you are interested in buying. So their mailing address is an address different from the "subject property".

There are also "out of town owners". Do not confuse the two because an absentee owner does not necessarily means that the person lives out of town. An absentee owner could live on the next street over, however an out-of-town owner could live out of state and it could've been months or years since they last saw the property. These people may still have a mortgage balance on the property or they could own it free and clear.

Each situation will differ. Personally, I like working with homeowners who own their properties free and clear because I find that they are more flexible on terms.

Before you spend time and money on any mailing campaigns here's what you need to know: Make sure you know in advance the areas that you want to buy your properties in as well as the price range and the type of properties that you are looking for, so that you can narrow your search and focus your marketing efforts effectively. I would advise that you initially focus on single-family homes and 2 to 4 family dwellings, because those types of properties will be easier and quicker for you to sell in the beginning, especially if you build your network of investors as I suggested in this book. However, you have to do what works for you based on your own plan, your investing strategy and your own available resources.

If you want your mailing campaigns to bring you good results, the most important thing you need to do is to be consistent with it and continuously send out letters to these owners. You can't just send out a letter or postcard once and forget about them. You have to consistently keep your name in their mind. This means that you have to have to send out your letters and postcards to them repetitively. You may not get a call from the first letter you send, but after the 3rd or 4th or even 8th letter their situations may change. If they have been consistently receiving your letters and postcards they will most likely contact you first when they become more motivated to sell. Life happens and people's situations change on a daily basis. I will go into more details about what types of situations make a seller motivated later. But consistency keeps you ahead of your competition.

The truth is that there is so much more you need to know in order to successfully run a direct mail marketing campaign. This is why I have asked veteran real estate investor and marketing expert Sharon Vornholt if she would allow me to post her articles about direct mailings on my blog and she was kind enough to let me share them with you. Her series of articles are the best that I have seen on the topic. To learn more about direct mailing, go to my website and check out the articles written by Sharon Vornholt. These articles will teach you from beginning to end how to run your direct mail campaigns to get the best results. www.SandyCesaire.com/directmailcampaigns.

Driving For Dollars

Drive around in the neighborhoods where you would like to invest in. Keep an eye out for potential deals.

Another way to find properties is to just get in the car and drive around. You can pick a specific time that works for you and the neighborhoods you want to drive through to look in. If you don't like driving around, don't have the time, or don't want to drive through neighborhoods alone, you can get someone else to do it for you. You can train another person how to identify the type of properties you are looking for and they can bring you back the information you need. If you have children that are old enough and wouldn't mind doing this for free or for a minimal fee, pay them to do it for you, or hire someone you know that could use a few extra bucks or even work out some kind of trade or agreement with them.

The bottom line here is this: if this is something that you don't like to do, that's ok, get someone else to do it for you. If you are not in the best financial situation to pay someone to help you and you are on your own, then guess what? If you are really serious about changing your current situation, accept the fact that you are going to have to do a lot of things that you may not like to do, at least until you can change the reality of your current financial situation. You gotta do what you gotta do to get the results that you want so that you can create the life that you want.

If you are driving around looking for deals, there are a few things you need to look out for. In fact, whenever you are driving anywhere, you should always be on the lookout for the following things, because deals are everywhere. Just be ready to act on them when you find them.

For Sale By Owners (Fsbo's)

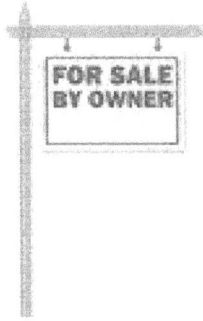

The next "for sale by owner" signs you see on someone's property could be your next deal. Call the owner and make that deal happen.

FSBO's is an abbreviated term used to describe properties that are for sale by the owner. Many homeowners will start off trying to sell their house themselves before they hire a real estate agent because they want to avoid paying 6% for a real estate commission. They want to see if they can find a buyer by themselves first. One thing you do need to be aware of when dealing with FSBO's is that there are some homeowners that hear the word "investor" and they can think we're out to take advantage of them. They think we are looking to beat them down on the price. Some people have their guard up immediately just because they think someone is out to get them, even when it isn't true.

Please understand that some of them feel that way simply because some people have felt they have been taken advantage by investors. But on the other hand, just as many homeowners have gotten the help they needed from an investor. There are certain scenarios where only an investor can help the homeowner. However, it is unfortunate when one investor acts unscrupulously because it reflects on the rest of us, even the good guys. Just be ready because this could be an objection that you may have to overcome with your potential sellers. My advice is to be up-front and honest. You are an investor and you are in this business to make money. I personally don't hide that, and really, most homeowners can understand this. Justify your lower-priced offers with your findings from your research and due diligence.

So when you run across these for sale by owner signs while you are out driving around, write down their information and contact them. If there is a potential deal there, make an appointment to go take a look at the property. Then, do your research and negotiate a good deal, secure it with a contract, market to find an end buyer or do a joint venture with another wholesaler who has already have buyers in place, let your title company or attorney handle the title work, close the deal and collect your check. It's a simple as that!

Properties For Rent

Landlords are both potential buyers and sellers. When you see a "for rent" sign call the number to find out if they are interested in selling or buying more properties.

For rent signs can serve two purposes for you. Each for rent sign you come across represents a potential buyer and a potential seller. Landlords are investors. Many of them own multiple properties and could be looking to buy more properties to add to their portfolio. Secondly, a landlord could also be interested in selling one or more of the properties that they already own, even a property they are actively advertising for rent.

Personally, there are properties that I choose to repair, rent out and afterwards put it up for sale as a cash-flowing turnkey property. The reason for doing certain deals that way is because I can charge more for the property. But guess what? If I get a call from a serious buyer responding to my for rent sign, I'd definitely be open to working out a deal that makes sense and is profitable for me.

Landlords are usually more open to working out an owner financing deal because they are interested in the monthly cash flow. In an ideal owner-financed scenario, the landlord (owner) benefits because they can still collect their monthly income from the property without having the worry of ongoing maintenance and extra costs such as property taxes, etc. A few years ago I called a "for rent" sign, and it turns out that the owner had several properties in the area and recently moved out of town so he was open to selling. I worked out a deal with him and bought that property with no money down. So when you see "For Rent" signs call them to find out if they would be interested in selling (and buying).

Distressed Properties

Property that shows physical signs of distress such as damaged roof, overgrown grass, broken windows and doors, could be a potential deal. Locate the owner, call or send them a letter to make a deal.

When you come across run down, vacant, abandoned properties, take down the address, look up the owner's information and send them a letter. Tell them that you are interested in buying their property and ask that they call you if they would like to sell. This works. Even when there are no for sale sign in front of the property, people's situations change all the time. While they may not be in a position to sell today or may not even want to sell; 3 months, 6 months, or even a year later they could be in an entirely different situation. Life can be somewhat unpredictable. People can go from extreme comfort to desperate within a blink of an eye.

As I was driving around in a neighborhood where I was rehabbing a property, I noticed a few properties that looked abandoned. So I sent letters out to them, and I got great responses, but there was one particular property where the homeowner called me almost a year later. It actually turned out that I had mistakenly sent the letter to that house because it was a very nice home that did not need repairs. In fact, the owner had just completed some upgrades to the property and was still living in the house. But months later, their situation changed. Their daughter became ill and they needed to move to be closer to the daughter to help take care of her. These owners had not planned on moving out of the house or selling that soon, but life happens!

Even though I sent that letter out to these owners by mistake, it's a perfect example of how people's circumstances can suddenly change. The fact is this: Bad things do happen to good people, and you as an investor can literally help improve someone else's life while being paid for it.

Pay attention to properties that are poorly maintained and show signs that they need moderate or major repairs. That may be a sign that the homeowner is having financial difficulty and cannot afford to pay for repairs or proper upkeep of the property. Send the owner a letter.

I would like to note that just because a property is being poorly maintained, that is not always a sign of financial difficulty, it could be a sign of physical difficulty.

I was once referred to an amazing older woman by a hard money lender who said I should see her house. I found out by talking to her that her tenant had moved out a few months ago and she was no longer in a position to maintain the property so she wanted to deed the property back to her lender.

When I met her for the first time, I arrived to the property before she did and I was waiting on the porch. Then comes this lady driving up to the property in a Mercedes Benz; she parks the car, turns off her ignition, gets out of the car, and I'm looking at her thinking to myself, Wow! Her arms look kind of short for her height.

She was fairly tall, between 5'7 and 5'8, hair styled short, dressed in her office clothing as if she was coming from work and carrying her designer handbag. So the closer she got to me while I was sitting on the porch, the more I came to realize that this woman did not have any arms. Both her arms were cut off at the elbow. I was stunned! Not because she had what we would call a "handicap", but because she was able to drive that car straight, parallel park straight, take the key out of the ignition, open and close the car door, pick up her purse, throw it on her shoulder then come up to the porch and unlock the door - all this with half an arm and without no hands or fingers.

I was amazed, and her attitude was incredible. I just had to ask her how it was that she could have such a good spirit with all that she is dealing with, so we began talking. While talking with her, I also found out that her biggest problem was that she did not have the help she needed to maintain the yard and upkeep the property. She explained to me how her husband had gotten into an accident and lost both of his legs and so now, even he could not even help maintain the yard anymore.

She had a tenant living in the property for almost 10 years but the tenant had to move out because her 9 year old daughter had a serious medical condition that required her to move elsewhere to get better care for her child. So all in all, this property had become too much for her to handle, physically, and that is why she was looking to turn the property back over to her private lender.

So the point is that there are so many different circumstances that can create a "distressed" situation. It could be financial, physical, mental, health; basically name it and it could be a potential problem. Now that we have this covered, let's move on.

Marketing Your Properties For Sale

ABM-"Always Be Marketing" Leads are the lifeblood of your business. You cannot survive without them.

Once you have access to properties that you can market and sell whether it is properties you secured on your own or through a JV partner, you need to know how to find the buyers to sell them to. Just as there are ways to find properties both online and offline, there are also several ways you can market your properties online and offline. If you have limited funds, the most inexpensive but effective way you can market properties offline are by using bandit signs and passing out flyers and posters at your local investor meetings. You can also do targeted direct mailing as well to locate buyers for your properties.

SELLING YOUR PROPERTIES OFFLINE

It is important to use a good mixture of both online and offline marketing tactics when marketing your properties to increase your chances of selling quickly.

In addition to bandit signs and flyers, which we discussed earlier, there are several other offline marketing strategies that you can use to market yourself, your business and properties for sale. You can do "bench advertising" or newspaper advertising, in addition to doing some television, radio and billboard advertising as well. If this type of advertising will work for you, go right ahead. But keep in mind that these types of advertisements require that you invest quite a bit of money to get started. The truth is that you won't know if it works until you try it.

You can still sell your properties and make a lot of money just by using other forms of advertising and networking strategies that I share with you in this book.

THE QUICKEST WAY TO SELL YOUR PROPERTIES

If you are just starting out, and you do not have buyers, one of the quickest ways to sell (if not THE quickest way) for you to find a buyer for your deal is by co-wholesaling or J-V (joint venture) with people who already have buyers lined up.

If you know any real estate agents that work with investors, you can offer them a commission on a non-exclusive agreement if they bring you a buyer. In other words, you are not listing the property with an agent, but you can agree to pay them a commission or flat fee if they bring you a buyer for the deal. Go back and revisit the section on working with an investor-friendly real estate agent. These are just a few examples.

Bandit Signs

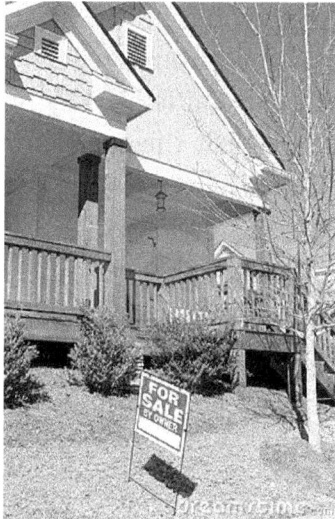

Bandit signs in front of your properties and throughout the neighborhood is a great way to find and build your buyers list. The people who call those signs are interested in buying in that area.

We covered bandit signs earlier in the section that's focused on how to find deals. But, let's talk about how they can help you market and sell your properties too.

The bandit signs you can use to market your properties are basically those blank 18X24 corrugated plastic (also called "coroplast") street signs. You may have seen them around your town. You can use these signs to advertise your properties by placing them in front of the property and at the corners of the different intersections within the neighborhood the property is located in. You will have to hand-write the property details on each sign, so you are going to need a big permanent marker like one of those "Magnum" Sharpie markers. The signs are only but so big, so be careful not to place too much information on it. You want it to be legible so that people that are driving by can actually read your sign, and most importantly, they can read your phone number.

Do NOT put the address of the property on the signs. You want people to call you to ask for more information. This gives you the chance to sell that person something. And even if they are not interested in the property that they called you on, you now have the opportunity to sell them another one of your properties.

You can be as creative with these signs as you want, but if you are advertising a property, there is certain information that you will definitely want to highlight, such as the number of bedrooms and bathrooms, the square footage and your phone number. You also may want to include any other features about the property that could attract potential buyers such as a pool, garage, an oversized yard, central heat & air (CHA), Concrete Block (CB) construction, as well as if the property is in move-in ready condition or if it is turnkey and cash-flowing. You can highlight anything else that would be considered a hot selling point. Use your judgment here.

Also, because there are many different types of properties, you may want to specify if the property is a duplex, triplex, quadplex, mobile home, or whatever type of property it is.

Every weekend, diligently put out your bandit signs to market your properties. If you don't have a property of your own to market, ask another investor or wholesaler if you can market any of theirs. You want to place those signs within 1-to-2-mile radius of the property in the neighborhood where it is located.

You can purchase bandit signs on sites such as www.cheapsigns.com. I list other websites at the end of this book where you can purchase bandit signs. Ask other investors for recommendations of places where you can locally buy these bandit signs with the stakes that go into the ground to hold the signs upright. Either yellow or white signs are fine because both of them work. You can search Google for places to buy these signs. You can also search Craigslist and eBay for people that may have signs that they want to get rid of. You could potentially buy them at a huge discount.

If you are on a budget, you can buy the signs and then cut them in half the long way. Actually you don't even have to be on a budget to do this; I do it all the time. If this is something you choose to do then for an extra $5 or $10 bucks you can have the sign company precut them for you. I made the mistake of doing it myself before, and it was an ABSOLUTE Nightmare.

The recommended time to put out bandit signs is Friday after 4pm or 5pm because that is when the sign police (code enforcement) are gone home for the weekend. Take the signs down on Sunday evenings before they are back to work.

Now here is A Quick Warning: The city can potentially fine you. That is why you want to have the signs out on the weekends when the enforcement officers are off-duty. Some cities are more vigilant than others when it comes to enforcing those rules. This is something else you can inquire from your fellow investors when you start networking. Find out what their experiences are or have been like with putting out bandit signs and find out just how strict the sign polices are in your city.

Chances are the people that call you after seeing your signs are already interested in buying in the neighborhood where you placed that sign. When you get calls from these potential buyers, there are a few questions you want to ask them. Keep in mind that you are not only trying to sell a property, you are also building your buyers list so if you find out you are talking to an investor, you want to get this person's information so you can add them to your list. You want to make sure you ask them about their buying criteria, and find out what type of properties they are looking to invest in. I have a questionnaire for you that you can download from my website. The link for that is at the end of the book.

SandyC Suggest Now that you are marketing yourself all over the place, both online and offline, you definitely do not want every stranger to have access to your personal cell phone number and you may not want to own two cell phones. With hard times most people cannot afford two cell phone bills, but there is a solution. Google has a service called "Google Voice" where you can get a local phone number and you are able to receive calls and place calls within the Google voice application that you can download onto your cell phone or your PC. With this service, you can forward calls to your cell phone, home phone, and even over to an answering service if you use one. You can send and receive text messages to and from both your cell phone and email account. You can even receive voice mails, you even have Caller-ID to capture the numbers for all your received or missed calls. This could be a great tool to for your business to capture leads and take business related calls. The best part about all of this is it's all absolutely FREE.

Go to www.google.com/voice to find out more about Google Voice and learn about all of their features. If you want to learn how to use these services check out their training tutorials at http://www.google.com/googlevoice/about.html

Selling Your Properties Online

There are dozens of ways you can market yourself and your real estate business on the Internet. Your personal website is only one of the ways. Learn how to take full advantage of the Internet to buy and sell more properties.

There are many online strategies you can use to market your deals. You can use online classified ad sites such as www.craigslist.com, www.backpage.com, and property listing sites like www.postlets.com where you can list all of the properties you are marketing for sale. Postlets is awesome because it gives you a free website to list your properties.

For each property you list on Postlets, it automatically syndicates that page to other websites like Zillow and many more real estate related websites all over the Internet, which help get your properties in front of more potential buyers. You can even post ads on craigslist and Backpage directly from Postlets by copying and pasting the embed code created by Postlets and your craigslist ad will look just like the generated flyer/webpage from Postlets. It's a wonderful platform to use for your real estate business and the best part is that all of this is available for Free.

You can connect your social media profiles to these websites and feed information to and from there as well. You can even video tape your properties exterior and interior, upload them to video sharing sites like www.youtube.com and share those videos on your social media pages.

The more exposure you can give to your properties and even yourself, the better, because this will help you attract buyers. Some of those buyers are career real estate investors with cash that are ALWAYS ready to buy. Once you make that connection, you will have an opportunity to market your properties to them over and over again.

SandyC Suggest I want you to know that your marketing activities will also help you build your buyers' list. Therefore, you will eventually need to purchase an email marketing software/system to organize your buyer contacts and automate the marketing process. For each call you receive from prospective buyers, make sure you get their names, email address, and phone number. The reason why you want this information (and you want to keep it organized) is because for the next property you are selling, you will be able to send a bulk email with the details of deal and the property info to all of your buyers at once.

There are several online systems that you can use for email marketing. Investors normally have no problem giving you their info because they are always looking for good deals to buy. I use www.verticalresponse.com to email deals to my buyers list and I also use www.aweber.com for my Internet marketing business. You can use Aweber as well to email info about your properties to your buyers. There are other websites such as www.constantcontact.com, www.icontact.com and several others, but the ones I'm sharing here are the ones that either I personally use, or personally know someone that use them. You can look more into these email marketing software options yourself.

Most of them offer a free 1-month trial period, however they do require a monthly fee to continue service. The fees are usually based on the size of your list. Since you are starting fresh, your cost would be on the lower end, but as your list grows, the fee will increase as well. Visit the websites to check out pricing; enrolling in one of these online email-marketing systems is worth the investment, but you can also use your regular email when you are first getting started to send out emails to multiple recipients at one time. Just remember to blind copy (BCC) the emails you are sending, otherwise everyone else attached to that email will see the others who are getting your emails as well.

Every time you receive a call from a prospective buyer, make sure you get their names, email address, and phone number. You want to keep it organized using the methods we discussed above. Because after awhile, you will be able to email the details along with pictures of your properties to everyone on your buyers list at once as opposed to emailing each person individually. However as you grow and determine who your "A" buyers are, I do recommend that you call your "A" buyers to personally tell them about the deal. You may sell that property with a phone call.

Those email-marketing systems normally keep "analytics" for each email campaign that you do. You can view how many people open each email, who clicks on any links included in your email, and the people who have not yet opened their email. You can call up your top investors who have not had the opportunity to see your email, but could possibly be interested in the deal you are marketing.

Creating A Win-Win Situation With Your Seller

Real estate investing is a business that creates an opportunity to make money by solving other people's problems.

Remember, YOU ARE A PROBLEM SOLVER. Before you make an offer to a seller, you must find out exactly what it is they REALLY want out of the deal and what their true motives for selling are.

You want to get to their underlying issues and worries. What are they looking for? Most sellers are going to give you a price and tell you a specific dollar amount out that they want to walk away with out of the sale, but often times, what they really want is deeper than just some dollar amount. I discussed this earlier in this book. Find out the problem or problems they are trying to solve by selling that property. If they are selling because they need the money, find out the reasons why they need money. What current or future problems will that money solve for them? If they are selling because the property has become a problem for them, find out the reasons why that property is now a problem. Get as many details as you can. You are flexible as an investor; this is something you will learn more about. The more you know about the problems (or pain) they're running away from and the 'reward' (solution) they are running toward, the better you can structure a deal that works out both for you and your seller and increase your chances of making an offer that will get accepted.

Every deal is different, so you have to approach them differently. As I mentioned before, create a win/win situation. This does not necessarily mean that the seller is walking away with a fist full of cash. A win-win for your seller could mean that you're getting rid of a major headache or problem property for them. That's a big win for someone who is truly frustrated with and tired of dealing with ongoing repairs, problem tenants, problem partners, a divorce, code enforcement violations, or any number of other problems that they could be facing. So when you are negotiating with a seller, remember that a 'win/win' situation does not necessarily mean that the seller is walking away with money immediately or even in the future.

With that said, when negotiating with sellers, you always, always, always have to look at the numbers and make sure they make sense. You are in business to make money. Don't forget it!

The Anatomy Of The Deal: Do The Numbers Work?

Real estate is a numbers game. Do the numbers work?

There is one thing you absolutely need to know before you rush out and start looking for properties. You need to learn how to analyze your deals. Real estate is a numbers game and I don't just mean that in the sense of cold calling and telemarketers or in the sense of sending out 200 mailers, expecting to get 5 leads that may end up being 1 deal.

When I say "numbers game", I am telling you that this real estate business of investing is literally a numbers game - meaning that you also have to buy the property at the right price because THAT number IS the deal. It does not matter how awesome the property is, if you don't get your numbers right, you don't have a deal. Period!

Depending on your exit strategy or the best plan for that deal, you have to make sure that the purchase price, the repair costs, plus the money it will cost to maintain and market the deal makes financial sense, whether it is coming out of your pocket or not!

If you don't have those numbers right, you're going to have a hard time selling or moving that property and you could end up being stuck with a property that you never intended to keep. What's worse is that as a beginner, you most likely won't have the money to close on the property yourself, so you could risk ruining your reputation by backing out of deals. This is especially true if you are dealing with other industry folks like real estate agents and investors. The real estate investing community is small and word gets around quickly. You don't want to become known for backing out of deals. So it is essential that you learn how to analyze your deals correctly and make sure the numbers work before you even make an offer. Let's briefly go over that here.

Now picture this:

You found a property. The seller is very motivated to sell. From your perspective they seem desperate. You may not even know what the real story is with them just yet, but you know one thing is for sure. They want to sell badly. They give you a price, and as a new investor, you are excited. You feel like you are so close to getting your first deal, you start doing that "hot pants dance".

Not every deal is a good deal, work your numbers before you commit. If the numbers don't work and the seller isn't motivated to lower the price, walk away!

Congratulate yourself for all the work you have done to get you this far, but this is the time where you need to compose yourself. Do not make the mistake of letting your emotions take over, because you need to focus on the logistics of the deal.

You must ask the right questions, and most importantly, you have to be certain that the numbers work before you take another step. Is the price right? Do the numbers work? Wait, what does that question even mean, "Do the numbers work"? Let's talk about that.

There are several factors such as closing fees, finance charges, attorney fees, repair and renovation costs, that can affect "the numbers" in a deal. You also need to take ongoing property taxes, insurance, and holding costs into consideration.

And first and foremost, you need to know the property value and how much profit or return you are looking for out of that deal. You have to look at all of these factors so you can negotiate the best price and terms for that deal.

Also, if you or your end-buyer are going to rehab the property to resell, you need to consider the cost to sell such as real estate commissions you will have to pay if you choose to use a Realtor to list and sell the property for you. There are other potential fees such as appraisal fees, inspection fees and a number of unforeseen costs as well.

When you are ready to resell the property, you will have to pay closing cost as the seller. You have to pay a prorated portion of the property taxes at closing and you may or (may not) have to help the buyer with their closing cost to get the deal closed.

That is something that needs be negotiated up-front, but your decision to pay the buyer's closing costs will depend on how motivated you are to sell, and it will also depend on the amount of demand you have for your property. Outside of the unforeseen costs, you can get a pretty close estimate of these fees upfront so you can "work the numbers" and analyze your deal.

Out of all of the costs that I have just mentioned, most are definite and some are only "potential" costs and may vary depending on the purchase price and on your plans for the property. Therefore when you are evaluating "the numbers", you have to know your exit strategy. Another way you can look at it is by asking yourself "what are the best possible exit strategies" based on the scenario of that deal.

As a beginner, you don't have to be an expert at estimating repair cost. Solicit the help of General Contractors and/or handymen until you get the hang of it.

Let's examine this scenario as an example:

If I am buying a property that I intend to keep as a long-term rental, the first thing I am going to do is inspect the property. Next, I will get quotes from a handyman or General contractor because I need to know how much money I have to put into that property to repair it and get it into livable (move-in) condition. I will find out upfront how much the property taxes are and how much the property insurance is going to cost me.

I'm also going to ask the owners, "How old is the roof?" because I need to know how long I have before I'm going to need to replace it (that could be months or years). I also need to know if I can sell the property at a reasonable price and still make a profit if I sell it without replacing that roof.

The same thing applies for all other potential major repairs the property may need. And even if plumbing, electrical and the other major concerns of the property seem perfect, I don't jump for joy just yet, because those things being ok doesn't necessarily mean that there aren't any other issues that could exist. I don't say this to scare you; I say it so you can be aware and beware. There can be a lot of unforeseen problems when you buy a property so you always need to keep that in the back of your mind. This is especially true when you are dealing with older properties and wood-framed properties.

Now, if I am going to keep this property as a rental, I want to know how much I can charge for rent. So I will investigate that. I want to know what the maximum is that I can charge for rent, not just the average. In my area, you can typically get more money in rent for section 8 tenants. That is one of the benefits of renting to section 8 tenants in addition to the guaranteed rent you receive from the government. I am a fan of renting to Section 8 tenants, however some investors avoid Section 8 at all costs. Hey, to each his own.

Perhaps the fact that I grew up in the housing projects myself makes me a little less biased towards section 8 tenants, or maybe not. But here's what I know as a fact: Section 8 or not, there are bad apples everywhere, in every class, in every group, in every community.

So here's another tip to help you maximize your rental income: If you are buying a property, let's say a 3bed/1bath that you can rent for $900-950 per month just as it is, but a 3bed/2bath in the same neighborhood will get you $1200 to $1250 per month in rent. I'd say you should add the 2nd bathroom. Obviously, you have to take into consideration the cost to add the 2nd bathroom. This is one of those occasions where networking with the right people can save, and make you money. As a newbie, you could potentially pay a contractor $7,000 or more to add a small bathroom onto your rental property, that should have cost you no more than $2,500 to $3,500 with proper permits. And even if it costs you $5,000, you don't want to find out through the "grapevine" later that one of your investors could have hooked you up with his contractors who would have only charged you a few thousands of dollars less for the same amount of work with permits. By the way I do advise you to get applicable permits when they are necessary BEFORE you begin any work. It can save you a lot of headache. Literally!

Taking all of this into consideration, the bottom line that you need to understand is if a $2,500-$3,500 upgrade will add another $300 or more to your monthly cash-flow, then that is well worth it because you can increase the return on your investment with the increased rental rate, and plus, the upgrade adds value to the property. Both homeowners and renters prefer 2 bathrooms. This makes it easier for the landlord to rent the property and collect more rent money. Properties with 2 bathrooms are much easier to sell as well.

To find out how much a property can rent for go to https://www.rentometer.com/. You can use www.Zillow.com as well for rent comparables.

This is just one way of looking at this situation, but what I need you to understand here is that even if you are wholesaling a property and you have no intention of keeping it for yourself, you still need to assess each deal the way that your buyers would. This is why it helps to know what your buyers are looking for and how they evaluate their deals.

So, it doesn't matter whether you plan on keeping the property or selling it. You still need to know all the facts and all the numbers. When you call or email your investors, you need to be prepared to tell them all the details about the deal including how much they can sell the property for, what's the minimum and maximum amount of rent they can charge, and how much money they will have to invest in repairs to get that property into "move-in ready" condition. Your investors will still do their own due diligence but this will get them interested enough to take a look at the deal. These are the habits that will help you move your properties quickly to your investors and end-buyers.

EVALUATING COMPARABLES

One of the most important factors in evaluating and determining the right price for a property includes evaluating comparables, often referred to as "comps" by real estate professionals. The Comparable properties that you use in your evaluation should be similar to the one you are buying (the "subject" property).

To be more accurate, the comps should be similar in size (square footage), age, overall condition, sold within the last 6 months, and in close proximity to the "subject" property. The distance between your comps and your "subject" property should be within a mile unless you have a valid reason to go beyond that. Otherwise, keep it under a mile.

Now, in addition to knowing what the similar properties have already sold for, it's also important to know the current listing or asking prices of similar properties that are available for sale in that neighborhood. Knowing this information is important and essential to how you price your OWN deals because THOSE properties are your competition. If I am looking to buy a property in any neighborhood and I have a choice between two similar properties, I will choose the one with better price and/or terms.

You can use websites such as www.zillow.com and www.realquest.com to check comparables yourself. You can also enlist the help of a real estate agent who has access to the MLS to run comps or do a "comparative market analysis" (also known as CMA) for you.

Here's a breakdown of how you can use Zillow: Once you are on the main page of www.Zillow.com, enter the property address that you are looking to get the comps for. The property details will come up, and you can then click on the link with the property address. Then on the next page if you look on the right hand side at the sidebar and scroll down, you will see a box designated as "Nearby Similar Sales". From there, you want to scroll down a tad bit and you will see a link that reads, "See sales similar to..." click on that hyperlink. On the next page, Zillow will show you a list of recently sold properties with similar features that are within 1 to 2 miles of the property you are evaluating.

You want to pay special attention to the distance each property is from the subject property. Only use the properties that are located within 1 mile away or less. Next, look for similarities between your subject property and the comparable such as square footage, number of bedrooms and bathrooms, year built, lot size and exterior construction.

It is crucial that you pay special attention to the date sold. The date the comparable properties were sold is important because it tells you the current market prices and a fair market value for similar properties. If the property was sold 12 months ago, most likely it's not going to do you much good, especially if your end-buyer is getting financed through a traditional lender.

Most lenders will not allow a property that was sold more than a year ago to be used as a comparable unless there is some sort of special circumstance, in which case they may decide to make an exception. But I would not count on it.

Be cautious not to use faulty comps because not only could they affect the perceived value of the property, it will also negatively affect your sales prices. You don't want to be 20 days into your transaction only to find out that you have to slash your price because the property value determined by an appraiser came out lower than your asking price and of course lower than you expected. Mistakes like this can eat up your profit, not to mention the time you will have wasted if the deal falls through.

SandyC Suggest: Here's one thing to keep in mind for your "fix & flip" buyers, since their retail buyers are likely to go through the traditional route for financing. Some lenders may require that the sold comps used be within less than a year, even though the average time span allowed is one full year. Beware of properties in areas where there aren't many comps. You or your investor may end up getting stuck with a property that you had no intention of keeping. When I evaluate properties I want to buy, I look for comps within half a mile and sold within the last 6 months. This is important because the after repair value (ARV) that you and your investor predetermined is based on those comparables.

Warning About Zillow

While Zillow can be a great resource for you, be careful about how you use the information that Zillow provides.

Zillow has become a very popular tool that investors use to research property values and comparable sales. There are a number of ways you can use Zillow to your advantage, but when you are the one doing "the buying", be very careful about using the data you pull from Zillow. You have to know the tricks on how to use Zillow properly. If you only use the generated estimated property value (aka Zestimate) that Zillow gives you as solid estimation of value when you are computing your numbers, you could end up overpaying for a property.

Let me give you an example. There is a neighborhood here in Tampa that anybody that lives here (investors and non-investors alike) would consider a war zone. At a time when properties were selling at an all-time low, properties in that neighborhood were selling in the teens and if they were in good condition and located on a slightly "better street" within that neighborhood they would go for lower 20's. I looked up a property in that same neighborhood on Zillow. It was a 4 bedroom/1bath block home. Although this property at the time was worth no more than $22,000 to $25,000, Zillow had the estimated property value at $71,000.

Now someone who is not familiar with the area would look at this as a good deal if someone offered it to them at $40,000 when in fact it was a horrible deal. Anyone who would have bought this property at that price would have dug a deep hole for themselves. If they would have been forced to sell that property, for any reason, during that time period, they would've ended up being $20,000 in the hole.

If you are looking to invest outside of your area or in markets that you are not familiar with, remember to do an extensive research and work with professionals or partners that knows that area well. Otherwise you could get yourself in some big financial troubles. Investigate before you invest.

You can still use Zillow as a research tool, as long as you're not taking their estimated values as final. The good thing about Zillow is they actually provide you a list of recently sold properties similar to the ones you are evaluating. You can check out these properties to see which one can be best used as comparables.

Also, the information that Zillow won't tell you is the condition the property was in when it was sold. It doesn't tell you if someone bought a property, fixed it up before they resold it or if they bought a property that needed extensive rehab and sold in that condition, as-is.

You may have to do some extra digging and use your judgment to figure this information out. Don't worry. Once you get to know your market, it will become easier for you to make these kinds of judgment calls. The best way to figure this out is to drive by these properties and even talk to the neighbors if you have to. But until you become a pro and are absolutely sure of what you are doing, you MUST verify everything.

Another way to find out this kind of information is to refer back to your county's real estate assessor's website. You can pull up the property record on these sites. It will give you the property's sales history as well as other information regarding the property.

When you are researching the info on the comparable properties, if you see that it was sold at a significantly lower price just 2 or 3 months prior (by the way, this may not necessarily be true), you could assume that the last person who purchased that property, renovated it and then resold it. You can always verify this by driving by that property as I mentioned before.

If you don't live in the same area as the property, get someone else to verify this information for you. A real estate agent may also be able help you with part of your due diligence as well. If you are buying in an area where there are plenty of comparables then your chances of making a costly error here decreases however, it is still very important that you perform your due diligence.

DETERMINING THE RIGHT OFFER AMOUNT

Here are two key points you need to consider when you are evaluating your deals, before you get to the "making an offer" stage. Other than the fact that each buyer has a different set of criteria and profits they want out of the deal, rehabbers and landlords look at their numbers and returns differently. So, I'm going to illustrate the way that rehabbers evaluate their

143

deals and the way landlords work their numbers. You will find that a landlord can typically pay more for the same property, while a rehabber would have to pay a lot less money for it.

So you need to keep the formulas that I'm going to show you in mind so that when you are evaluating your wholesale deals you will know how to structure the best deal and make an offer based on the end-buyer that you are targeting for that specific deal.

Rehabbers work their numbers based on the After Repair Value (ARV) of the property. This is because they need to know what they can sell that property to a retail buyer for after it is in move-in-ready condition. This is where all their profits are. Again, as I mentioned before, the profit that your investor-buyers expect will vary from investor to investor. However, in the real estate investing industry there is an overall formula that is used as a basis of determining the right price to pay for cash and rehabbed deals.

Now, before I go over the formula, I want you to remember that you have to make a profit as well so you have to figure in the amount of money you want to make on the deal, and also leave some "wiggle" room for negotiation.

Rehabbers typically look to buy their properties at 70% of the after repair value or better. If they are being funded through a hard money lender, 65%-70% of the ARV is normally acceptable by a hard money lender, depending on if the price range is more towards the higher or lower price levels. So let's say for example, a property's ARV is $300,000 and the property needs $40,000 in repairs. You have to calculate 70% of $300,000, which leaves you at $210,000. But you can't stop there because the property needs $40,000 in repairs to be brought up to living condition so that it can be sold to someone who wants to move in that property. So you now have to subtract the $40,000 from $210,000, which leaves you with $130,000. This number, if they are following the 70% rule, will be the highest price your investor will pay you for the property.

But wait a minute, what about your profit?

If the rehabber can only pay you $130,000 for the property, then you have to deduct the amount of profit you want to make. Not only that, there's a matter of closing cost. Let's assume this is an assignment deal so there is only one closing involved and you offered to pay for sellers closing cost as well. So all together, we'll say total closing is $3,000 (for simple numbers' sake) and you want to make $10,000 on this deal. This leaves you with an additional $13,000 that you have to deduct.

You're now left with $117,000. It's now time for you to make your offer to the seller and you have determined that in order for you to clear $10,000, the MOST you can pay for the property is $117,000. So in this case, you don't want to start your offer with $117,000 because there's a chance your seller may counter at a higher price, which will eat up a part of your profit. You want to start at $12,000 lower (you can use your own judgment), and if the seller accepts the lower offer then that's more money in your pocket! If they counter higher, you can potentially end up with the price that you were looking for.

Take the same approach but in reverse when you are negotiating with your buyers as well because the good ones will always ask you, "What the best can you do?" until you drop your price 3 times if you're not sharp with this. So keep this in mind at all times.

Landlords, on the other hand, evaluate their deals differently than rehabbers. Landlords or "buy & hold" investors rate the potential of their investments based on the cap rate and cash-on-cash return. The cap rate is basically a measure of the purchase price compared to the net income the property brings in. It lets them know if they are buying at a good price and getting a "good deal" on the property. This is entirely subjective, as we discussed throughout this entire book.

Cash on cash return, however, is a measure of how much cash you actually invest in the deal compared to how much money the property brings in. So, to keep this simple, let's say you get financing to purchase a property. You make a down payment of $30,000. The $30,000 is your actual cash investment. And that is the amount you would use to compare to the net income you make on the property to calculate your cash-on-cash return on this deal.

Remember that when you are paying all cash for a property, the cap rate and cash-on-cash return will be the same. Generally, the cap rate formula is what landlords use to determine how good of an investment a deal is.

Depending on your individual buyer and the market they are in, their expectations will differ based on their investment model. So I will attempt to keep this as simple as possible. You can do more research on this to learn how to work out these numbers. Before you can even calculate the cap rate and cash on cash return, you need to know the following formulas:

The Cap Rate Formula:

Annual NET Income / Purchase Price = Cap Rate

The Cash-on-Cash Return Formula:

Net Annual Income / Total Cash Invested = Cash-on-Cash Return

Net Annual Income Formula:

Monthly Rental Revenue - Monthly Expenses = Net Income

(Multiply net income by 12 months for annual income)

In order to calculate the cap rate and cash on cash return, you have to know how much rent the property is generating monthly or how much rent it can potentially generate. Remember you can use Zillow or https://www.rentometer.com to get rent comparables.

You also have to know the monthly expenses involved. Expenses include property taxes, property insurance, and maintenance. Some expenses may or may not apply to each property. These expenses are property management fee, HOA (homeowner's association). In addition, you have to account for vacancies.

Expenses such as monthly maintenance, repairs, and vacancies are not as easy to calculate up-front because there are many factors that affect those numbers. Therefore you have to make an educated guess. For example, a property that has been recently renovated will require less maintenance than a property that has not been updated in years. You have to use your judgment and what you have learned in these situations.

To keep things simple, when I do my calculation on properties that I am wholesaling, I only factor in property taxes and insurance. I leave the property management fee, maintenance, and vacancy up to my buyers to factor in for themselves because each of them do things differently and have different investing styles. Some investors are more hands-on with their rental properties and manage the property themselves, and sometimes tenants take care of repairs themselves, so expenses for them are lower than the investor who has to hire these jobs out.

Remember that your buyers will also do their own due diligence, but your initial calculation will give them a general idea if the deal is good enough for them or not. However, if you are buying the property for yourself or are certain of the buyer that you will sell that property to, I encourage you to factor in all expenses, provided you know their exact plans for that property.

The most important point in all of this is to approach your buyers to find out exactly what type of return they are looking for so that when you make offers to your sellers, you can make it a price where you can profit and your investors will cash flow and get the return that they want. **Remember: Working your numbers from these angles will increase your chances of selling your properties quickly.**

Finally, when you are making offers to your sellers to buy their property, they may ask you for a "proof of funds letter" to verify that able to make good on your promise to buy their home. So, you will have to provide proof of funds (POF), especially in cases when real estate agents are involved. A transactional lender is a good source to get your proof of funds letters (refer back to the section on transactional lending). However, if you have a partner with a substantial amount of cash in the bank, you can provide their bank statement as proof of fund as well to accompany your offer. If you are making offers on properties that are listed with a real estate agent, no one will take your offer serious if there is no proof of funds or some sort of approval letter or bank statement submitted with your offer. You have to show that you are a serious buyer. So keep this in mind when you submit your offers.

Closing Your Deals And Getting Paid

Ok so you have found a property to buy, and analyzed and evaluated the deal to make sure that the numbers work. You negotiated a good deal, got the property under contract with your seller and secured an end-buyer to purchase the property from you. The next thing you need to do is have an investor-friendly title company or attorney to handle the rest of the transaction and check out the title for you.

That means that they are going to perform a title search to look through the property's records to verify who the property owners are and to ensure that there aren't any unpaid mortgages, liens, judgments or claims against the property. If any of those issues come up on the title search, which you will often see throughout your real estate career, then you, the title company and the property owner just have to work together to get those liens cleared before closing.

You will run across endless unique situations that can cloud title throughout your real estate investing career. Most times those issues only delay closings. The delays could last anywhere from days to many, many months, but if the issues are workable you will have a big payday in the end.

After the title company completes the search (which should take 48 to 72 hours), the title company then issues an owner's title insurance policy, and if there is a lender involved, they issue a lender's policy as well. This insurance protects title of the property. It also protects the homeowner and the lender in the event that any title disputes, conflicts, or claims arise against the property in the future.

SandyC Suggest: I would also like to point out that if you have established a good relationship with your title company and you consistently send them multiple deals and leads, when the time comes and you need them to rush a deal, they may be able to do a rush and run title for you within 24 hours depending on their workload.

So what about closing costs? Closing fees and total closing costs vary from deal to deal. First of all, the sales price affects the total closing cost. Typically the higher the purchase price, the higher the closing cost will be because certain fees are based on a percentage of that purchase price.

Also each title companies and attorneys charge different fees for their services. Furthermore, a buyer's closing cost will vary based on whether they are paying cash for the property or getting financed, because there are more fees involved for financed buyers.

Typical closing costs involve charges for the title search, closing or settlement fee, owner's title policy, recording fees, transfer taxes, property taxes, and if there's a lender involved expect additional fees such as lender's title policy, underwriting fees, lender processing fees, prepaid interest, and homeowner's insurance (because lenders like for at least 6 months to a year homeowner's insurance to be paid in advance).

Depending on the deal there may be other fees such as Homeowner's Association (HOA) fee, survey fee, appraisal fee, credit report fee, courier fee, and wire transfer fee. Those are the main fees you may incur when closing a transaction.

Some fees, such as transfer taxes, are required to be paid by the seller and other fees are the responsibility of the buyer. In any case, any and all of these costs can be negotiated. You can offer to pay all of the seller's fees in addition to yours, as is the case of many wholesale deals. You can also negotiate and have the seller pay all of your closing cost. You will know what to do after you evaluate each deal and the situation surrounding the deal.

You should make it a habit to have your title company prepare an estimated HUD-1 document even before you get the property under contract. You have to know what these fees are so you can evaluate your deals, plus, your end-buyers and sellers will want to know what their costs are as well.

In wholesale deals it is common to offer to pay for all of the seller's closing costs so they can net the price they want or that you agreed to minus property tax proration. However, there will be several occasions where sellers will cover their own closing cost. Either way you need to know your fees up front.

Another important reason why you need to know the fees upfront is to make sure that your title company or attorney is not charging you outrageous fees. You can get estimated HUD-1 from at least 2 other title companies to compare the charges. If you have a title company that you really would like to work with but their fees are steep, simply ask them if they would be willing to match the fees from your best option. Obviously you want to use your judgment here and be reasonable, especially if this is a title agent that helps you with many other services for free and goes out of their way to make your deals work.

Build a solid relationship with your title agent or attorney because they can do so much for you beyond the typical closing duties. For example, when I need a Power of Attorney or a note and mortgage printed up, or even a Quit Claim deed, I just call my title agent to help me with these things and sometimes she'll even fill them out for me.

What's more, she will even do this for me if those documents have nothing to do with a deal we're working on! This is a relationship that we have nurtured for a decade. Also there will be times when you may need a notary for unrelated transactions and it's convenient to have someone that you can call to help you with that, even after business hours.

Like I mentioned earlier, your title company can provide you many more services such as mailing lists and other valuable data. For these reasons alone, you need to create a win/win relationship with your closing agents. You can help them by not only sending them your deals but you can refer your other investor friends that are actively closing deals to them as well.

It's good to have 2 to 3 good title companies that you constantly use in case you have a deal that needs to be closed immediately. There could be any number of valid reasons why they may not be able rush a deal for you. It's always great to have a backup if the others are tied up or if your agent goes on vacation.

The Key To Your Success In This Business

BE RESOURCEFUL BE CREATIVE

As we are reaching the last section of this book, I want to point out that if you take anything away from this book, it should be this: In order to be successful in this business you have to be resourceful, creative and people-oriented. You have to learn how to think outside of the ordinary. You don't have to be a people person, but must learn how to deal with people by listening to them. People want to know that they matter. You can be attentive and still be able to make your points.

Start reading psychology books, particularly the "psychology of human behavior" kinds of books, because this information will help you in your business (and in life in general). The bottom line is, you can learn all the strategies you want, but if you don't know how to be resourceful, if you don't know how to think outside of the box and think creatively, if you don't know how to deal with people, then you will not be successful in this business (let alone any other business) and you might as well kiss and makeup with your boss because that's who you will be spending the rest of your life with. Lol!

In this business most deals you'll encounter will be unique. Each of them also come with a unique set of challenges, and if you are not prepared to be flexible to adjust to each circumstance accordingly while thinking outside of the box, you will have a difficult time getting those deals closed.

You have to learn the basic fundamentals of each strategy, and real estate investing in general. Those fundamentals carry over from deal to deal, but everything else can be worked out. You have to learn how to be flexible and creative so that you can replace any element that becomes a challenge with a technique that works so you can get that deal closed. Your ability to be resourceful and think outside of the ordinary will help you make things happen. So you don't need money to make money in this business, but your mind and your resourcefulness are the two single most powerful tools you can have in your arsenal. With those two, you can win at anything.

With this in mind, you are now ready for the next phase, which really has to be your first phase. There is some very serious stuff you need to do before you jump into this business.

Creating Your Life Plan

Reflect on what it is you really want out of life and create a plan to achieve it.

As I mentioned at the beginning of the book, there is one thing that you absolutely need to do before you get started with your real estate investing career.

Well there are actually two things you need to do: You need to take time out and create two plans, a life plan and a business plan. They both will serve as a map for you to guide you and keep you on the right path to ensure that you successfully reach your desired goal. The business plan will be a guide as to how you will approach and run your business. Your life plan will focus on your personal life and will help you focus on what you want for your life.

Most people spend more time planning a vacation more than they do planning their own lives. They live from the day-to-day and let life happen to them instead of them taking control of what happens in their lives. They live in a routine world where they get up each day and let everything and everyone else around them dictate what they do with their day and how they do it and then they wake up one day wondering where did time go and do they have to show for it. They don't know happened and why they feel so lost, unfulfilled and unhappy.

This is what happens when you don't have a clear vision and a clear purpose for your own life. You allow everyone else to control the "what, how, where, when and why" of your life, starting with your boss.

Things don't have to stay this way. You can change this. To get out of this "rut" you have to start with a life plan: YOUR life plan. What do you want for YOURSELF? Envision it then write it down. Keep it with you daily to remind you to work on those things that will help you get what it is that you want out of life. And when you find yourself getting off track for whatever reason, you can also use it as a guide to get you back on track.

Your life plan should cover the answers to these questions:

- What matters to you the most in your life?

- What are your highest priorities?

Make a list of these things. If you're a religious or spiritual person and believe in God, you may have God as number one on your list then yourself, your spouse, your children, your family, your friends, your health, career, finances and anything else that is important to you. Identify those things write them down. Create a list.

The next step for you to do is **create a specific plan to achieve each of the things that are important to you** in your life. For every single one of those items you need to plan out the following:

- What is the desired outcome?

- What's the purpose?

- When it comes to God, yourself, your spouse, your children, family, friends, career,

- health and finances, where do you want to be?

- What is it that you're trying to accomplish?

The next thing you need to do is **picture what your life looks like when you have achieved what it is you want to achieve** for those items. So for example, picture that your health, finances, family life, etc. are at the level where you want them to be. What does that "life" look like? What is your life like when your income level reaches the point that YOU want? What does your relationship with your spouse and your children look like when you are able to spend more quality time with them, without outside distractions and without financial worry? **Write those things down as if you have already accomplished them.** Write it in the present tense. This is a way of *speaking your vision into existence.*

Next, you will examine where you are now in your life. For example, if God is important to you, then evaluate: What is your current relationship with God? How is your relationship with your spouse and your children now? Do you get to spend time with them? Are you able to provide for them the way you want to? How is your health? Are you consistently getting ill? Are you at the weight level that you desire? How's your diet, do you need to do better? How's your career going, and How are you doing financially? Are you always stressed due to lack of work or stressed because you are overworked, underpaid and hardly have time left for yourself and your family? Are you working a dead-end job?

For each of those items that are important to you, examine where you are in your life now with regard to each one of them. You have to **be brutally honest with yourself** and write these things down. This plan is for you and for you only so don't feel embarrassed about anyone seeing it unless you plan on sharing it with others. If you have someone that you trust to help keep you accountable, go ahead and share it with that person. Otherwise, keep it to yourself. **The important thing is you have to face the hard truth of your current situation before you can begin to change it. Period!**

This next step is one of the most crucial steps. This is where you will **create and write down the actual ACTION Steps that you must take that will get from your current situation to your desired outcome.** You have to do this for each of the items that are important to you. DO NOT combine any of the action steps for any 2 items. This part answers the "How" in your plan. This is HOW you will get from where you are to where you want to be. You have to be very specific about this if you are serious about achieving your goals and creating a life that you will love.

Take your time to create this plan. Remember that this is **YOUR plan**, so this has to reflect what you want for YOUR OWN LIFE, not what your mother, your father, your spouse, your friends or pastor or anyone else tell you that you SHOULD want for your life. **You have to go deep in your**

heart and your thoughts, *be honest with yourself* and design your own life map.

After you create this plan, do not set it aside and forget about it. You will need to review it regularly. Figure out the schedule that works best for you but for the first few months I recommend daily and then you can review it weekly to make sure you are on the right path to getting what you want. It is perfectly fine to modify this plan as you grow more into yourself and figure out certain things that you want or when something is no longer important to you or even if you just need to tweak some things.

The important thing is that *this is YOUR life and YOU are in control and now you can get in the driver's seat and decide what happens, where you going, and how you will get there.*

Creating Your Business Plan

Just as you are going to do in your life plan, in your business plan you should identify where you are, where you want to go and how you will get there.

Again, **YOU are in the driver seat and it is up to YOU to create a road map that will increase your chances of reaching success in your real estate business.**

Many times people look at business plans only as a tool to secure funding from banks and other lenders but even if you are starting off with your own money you still need to create a business plan because this will be the blueprint for how you will run and grow your business and you will have to refer back to this plan to track your progress.

There are tons of resources online that can guide you in creating a business plan. Check out my website for more on creating a business plan. The thing I want you to keep in mind here is to not be intimidated and focus on the following key points below.

Your plan should include your company information and the people involved, officers and/or partners. Even if you are a "one-man band" starting your business alone, write it down. What is everyone bringing to the table? What's their background and what experiences do they have? What is YOUR background and what experiences do YOU have? How will you structure your business? Will you incorporate or get set up as a limited liability or a sole proprietor?

I suggest you contact a CPA or an attorney with real estate investing experience to help you with this process. How much money will you need to start your business, or are you starting with no cash? Remember you need to know this so you can approach your business accordingly.

What are all the startup costs involved? Even if you are wholesaling real estate which is possible to do with little cash, there are a few items that cost money. For example, bandit signs cost money. It costs money to have access to the Internet. You still have to keep your lights on. You have to pay a phone company to keep your phone on. You're going to need that phone to place and receive calls to potential buyers and sellers and JV partners. You need a car and fuel to drive to and from properties. The car doesn't have to be yours but someone has to pay for the gas.

You need a computer and printer. You can get away without having a fax machine by scanning documents and using the e-fax services to send and receive fax but even those services cost money. You can also scan and email purchase and sales contracts to potential buyers and sellers but you may run across elderly sellers who do not even have an email let alone know how to use one. I know that I have experienced this situation on several occasions. This is not to discourage, I want you to think of these things ahead of time so that you can plan accordingly. Chances are you already have most those items already.

Will you hire a personal assistant? Will they work full-time or part-time? How much will you pay them, hourly, weekly, and monthly? What's your monthly marketing cost going to be? How much will you budget for business and personal development? Will you hire a coach or mentor to guide you and help you complete your transactions successfully? Write these things down in your business plan.

You should also include in your business plan your sales strategy, marketing strategy, and your acquisition strategy. How and where will you find your deals? What's your target market? What's your profit plan? How many deals do you want to do per year and how much do you want to profit per deal?

If you do need a deal funded, where will you get the money? Which lender or partner will be willing to fund a deal for you? Who will be on your team and what services do they offer? Who are your JV partners going to be? Do you have any challenges, and if so what are they and do you plan on overcoming them? And last but not least, what's your exit strategy? What is the end goal for your business? These are some of the things we have talked about previously.

Do more research on creating your business plan. You can find many business plan templates online. In my opinion, content is more important than having a fancy looking business plan that does nothing to help you stay on track to achieving your goals and becoming successful.

You need to be clear about the vision you have for your business and the actions you're going to take to make the vision a reality. Like the saying goes, "If you don't know where you're going any road will get you there" and even worse you may never get there.

Well, there you have it! We have reached the end of this book. I have shared with you tons of valuable information to help you get started off on the right foot. *If you start today, you can literally get your first deal done and put a few thousands of dollars in your pocket within the next couple*

of months, however it is more than possible to close your first deal in just 30 days or less.

Everyone's results will vary. Your result will be a direct correlation of the amount of time and effort you invest in yourself (through education) and the time you take to build your business.

So if real estate investing is what you really want to do, don't waste any more time. I have given you a very detailed guide to start from, so get off your butt and start accumulating some assets. Remember, Investigate before you Invest and Do The Work!

Now that you have finished this book, put on your business hat, and get to work!

Case Studies

Here are a few examples of wholesale deals that I have done. My goal here is to share different examples and scenarios of the type of deals I discussed with you throughout this book. Each deal and closing was unique and the buyers and sellers/properties were found using different techniques. I attempted to describe each one of them the best way I could to give you an idea of the types of "real life" wholesale deals you may encounter once you get started.

EXAMPLE DEAL 1

TRANSACTION TYPE:	Wholesale/Bank-Owned
LEAD SOURCE:	Driving-FSBO
CLOSING TYPE:	Assignment
HOW I FOUND A BUYER:	Bandit signs
BUYER FUNDING SOURCE:	Cash
PROFIT:	$5,000

EXAMPLE DEAL 2

TRANSACTION TYPE:	Wholesale/Short Sale
LEAD SOURCE:	Real estate agent
CLOSING TYPE:	Double Closing
HOW I FOUND A BUYER:	Wholesaler/Investor
BUYER FUNDING SOURCE:	Cash
PROFIT:	**$17,500**

EXAMPLE DEAL 3

TRANSACTION TYPE:	Wholesale/Short Sale
LEAD SOURCE:	Loan Officer
CLOSING TYPE:	Double Closing
HOW I FOUND A BUYER:	Called a current Investor
BUYER FUNDING SOURCE:	Cash
PROFIT:	$4,000

EXAMPLE DEAL 4

TRANSACTION TYPE: Wholesale/Short Sale
LEAD SOURCE: Realtor
CLOSING TYPE: Double Closing
HOW I FOUND A BUYER: Blast email to buyer's list-Multiple offers
BUYER FUNDING SOURCE: Cash
PROFIT: $13,000

EXAMPLE DEAL 5

TRANSACTION TYPE: Wholesale/Bank-Owned

LEAD SOURCE: Online   Bank-Owned   Property
Site

CLOSING TYPE: Double Closing

HOW I FOUND A BUYER: My Student found the buyer

BUYER FUNDING SOURCE: Cash

PROFIT: $7,000

EXAMPLE DEAL 6

TRANSACTION TYPE: Wholesale/Private owner

LEAD SOURCE: Realtor-Property was not listed

CLOSING TYPE: Assignment

HOW I FOUND A BUYER: Called one of my investors

BUYER FUNDING SOURCE: Cash

PROFIT: $7,500

EXAMPLE DEAL 7

TRANSACTION TYPE: Wholesale/Private owner

LEAD SOURCE: Driving around-FSBO sign

CLOSING TYPE: Assignment

HOW I FOUND A BUYER: Sold   to   one   of   my   investors

BUYER FUNDING SOURCE: Cash

PROFIT: $5,000

EXAMPLE DEAL 8

TRANSACTION TYPE: Wholesale/Bank-Owned

LEAD SOURCE: Online   Bank   Owned
Property Site

CLOSING TYPE: Double Closing

HOW I FOUND A BUYER: One of my Investors

BUYER FUNDING SOURCE: Hard money financing

PROFIT: $7,000

EXAMPLE DEAL 9

TRANSACTION TYPE:	Wholesale/Private owner
LEAD SOURCE:	Driving Around-FSBO
CLOSING TYPE:	Assignment
HOW I FOUND A BUYER:	Craigslist
BUYER FUNDING SOURCE:	Cash
PROFIT:	$3,500

EXAMPLE DEAL 10

TRANSACTION TYPE:	Wholesale/Bank-Owned
LEAD SOURCE:	Online
CLOSING TYPE:	Double Closing
HOW I FOUND A BUYER:	One of my Investors
BUYER FUNDING SOURCE:	Cash
PROFIT:	$3,500

Join us at <u>www.REICashIn30Days.com</u> "REI Cash In 30 Days System" Online Course for continuous support and training.

Summary

Here is a summary and action steps below you should be focusing on.

- Create your life plan and a business plan

- Get a designated business phone number on Google voice

- Order your business cards

- Get a domain name from Godaddy.com and Build your website

- Network at your local REIA meetings and on the internet social media

- Get your team of professionals together (title company, attorneys, wholesalers, realtors, lenders, etc.)

- Create an account on Postlets.com

- Locate and get in touch with the top wholesalers in your area

- Purchase bandit signs

- Start Co-wholesaling and marketing properties

- Generate buyers leads, focus on cash investors that buys multiple properties

- Generate motivated seller leads using methods discussed above

- Do your due diligence (Investigate and evaluate before you invest)

- Make offers on properties and get properties under contract

- Market your properties for sale using the methods discussed above

- Close the deal and Get Paid!

- Then call me to send me my cut (ok this is optional, lol)

SELLING PROPERTIES RECAP

- JV with wholesalers who already have a buyers list

- Sell to wholesaler who will pay cash and close before they even have a buyer

- Market and sell to other cash investors

- Send out a blast email and make personal calls to your buyers to tell them about the deal

- Realtor who work with investors- offer them a commission or a flat fee to sell your property to their buyers

- Advertise the property on various online classified sites such as craigslist, Backpages, etc.

- Create a Postlet profile for it on Postlet web page

- List it on your personal website if you have one (if you don't get one)

- Put out bandit signs

- Mail out postcards, flyers or letters to Cash investors who RECENTLY bought property in that neighborhood

- Advertise on social media, investors groups

Links and Resources

www.SandyCesaire.com

Real Estate Investor Association

http://www.nationalreia.com/

Business Cards

www.vistaprint.com

Classified Ads: Find For Sale By Owners Properties & List Your Properties For Sale

www.craigslist.com

www.backpage.com

http://www.forsalebyowner.com

http://www.ebayclassifieds.com

http://www.oodle.com

http://www.forsalebyowner.com

http://www.usfreeads.com

Bank Owned and Auction Properties

www.Hubzu.com

http://www.hudsonandmarshall.com

www.Auction.com

www.ocwen.com/reo

www.buybankhomes.com

www.homesales.gov

www.buybankhomes.com

www.homepath.com

www.bidselect.com

www.homestep.com

www.lendersreo.com

www.countrywide.com

www.southernreo.com

www.propertydisposal.gov

Privately Owned Investment Co. (Sells Discounted Properties)

www.econohomes.com

Nationwide MLS

www.realtor.com

HUD Properties

www.hudhomestore.com

Direct Mail Campaign Resources

www.ListSource.com

http://www.melissadata.com/

http://www.infousa.com/direct-mail/

http://yellowletterscomplete.com/

http://www.corelogic.com/

http://dataquick.com/

http://probatesdaily.com

Email Marketing (BLAST EMAIL)

www.verticalresponse.com

www.aweber.com

www.icontact.com

www.constantcontact.com

Free Online Property Listing for marketing and selling your properties

www.Postlets.com

www.vflyer.com

Post Your Property Video On These Sites and Drive Traffic To Them

www.Youtube.com

http://www.dailymotion.com/us

http://vimeo.com

Nationwide Title Search

http://netronline.com

Networking and Social Media Sites

http://www.meetup.com

www.LinkedIn.com

www.Facebook.com

Comparable Search

www.Zillow.com

www.Realquest.com (More accurate comps)

http://www.investorcompsonline.com/

http://www.findcompsnow.com/

http://www.redfin.com/

http://www.trulia.com/

Rent Comps

https://www.rentometer.com

www.Zillow.com

Keep up with industry news: Market research

www.realtytrac.com

Get Your Domain Name For Your Website

www.Godaddy.com

Free Local Phone Numbers and phone service

www.google.com/voice

Skip Tracing Services

http://www.findtheseller.com/

http://www.tlo.com/

www.anywho.com

http://www.spokeo.com

CRM

www.Zoho.com

Forms

Buyer Lead questionnaire.

Seller Questionnaire

Recommended Books

Rich Dad Poor Dad

The Richest Man In Babylon

Rich Dad's CASHFLOW Quadrant

Think and Grow Rich

Rich Dad's Conspiracy Of The Rich: The 8 New Rules Of Money

How to Win Friends & Influence People

Persuasion: The Art of Getting What You Want

Multiple Streams of Income: How to Generate a Lifetime of Unlimited   Wealth!

About The Author

My name is Sandy Cesaire and I'm a real estate investor.

From my last name, you can probably tell that I'm not a "natural born American". I'm from Port-au-Prince, Haiti, which is one of the poorest countries in the Caribbean.

I come from humble beginnings. When I was young, my father knew that the opportunities were limited in Haiti, so he obtained a Visa, and found seasonal employment in the farms in South Florida. He would travel back and forth from Florida to Haiti, all because he wanted something better for his family.

My mother eventually obtained a work Visa too and joined my father in the U.S. workforce. They were cheap labor in South Florida's agriculture industry. It came at a sacrifice because working in the States meant that they had to leave my sister and me behind in Haiti in the care of our aunts.

My parents settled in small Florida town called Belle Glade, which is just 80 miles north of Miami. The locals call Belle Glade Muck City. The sign that travelers see upon entering the city says, "Welcome to Belle Glade, her soil is her fortune." The business owners may have found fortune, but my father and mother found hard work.

My parents would work long days packing boxes of corn at ten cents per box. A day's earnings would be less than $40, and that's working 10 to 12 hours days. They would later find better jobs at a plant, where they were each made a whopping $4.25 an hour. That money had to stretch so they could survive in Florida, while also taking care of the family back home in Haiti. It was a difficult time but they persevered, as they were determined to reunite our family.

In 1990, when I was 9 years old, my parents' dream came true. They brought my sister and I to the USA, to Belle Glade, our new home. We lived in the housing projects with a few extras, and no luxuries, and I didn't even speak English. At times mom had to rely on welfare to make ends meet, and we scraped by with just enough to survive. I didn't come from money, but I always knew there was a better life out there. I had faith and dreamed that I would become successful one day.

I was blessed with a mother who noticed that I had an inner drive. She supported and encouraged me to pursue my passions. My parents at taught me that I had to work hard to achieve my dreams. There was a time when I thought I wanted to be a doctor, and I volunteered at our local hospital and dialysis center. I've always had an entrepreneurial spirit and also started a small beauty supply store and a cleaning business.

In 1999, at the ripe old age of 18, I left the fields of Belle Glade behind, and moved to Florida's "suncoast", also known as Tampa. I was hooked on the idea of being my own boss and I set my sights on making it a reality. That's how I found real estate, or maybe real estate found me. I think that the late night infomercial real estate guru had something to do with it because I certainly didn't know anyone who worked in real estate.

I decided to take a real estate course. I didn't have enough money to pay for the class up front so I went on a payment plan, and studied hard. I was looking forward to starting my career. There was one minor problem. When it was time to pay the final payment, I hadn't enough money to make the $45 payment. That meant that I couldn't finish the class, and I couldn't take the state license test.

I was disappointed for sure, but not defeated. I was haunted by my failure to complete the real estate licensing course the first time around, but deep down, I knew that real estate was my ticket to an independent and prosperous life. It took me two years to return to the real estate school, but this time around I wisely paid for the course up front. After I finished it, I passed the state exam on the first try! I was finally a Realtor, and six months after that I became a loan officer as well. Things were really looking up for the small girl who arrived in the USA from Haiti, who came here without any English skills.

I quickly realized that the people making the big bucks were investing in real estate. That was my next hill to climb.

I didn't know very much about the business of real estate investing, but I started going to investor meetings and networking with real estate investors to learn as much as I could from them. I didn't know anything in the beginning, but I figured out enough to get started. I also surrounded myself with mentors in the industry and continued my education by taking courses on different real estate investing strategies.

When I started out, I had no cash, no credit, and no property that could be used as collateral for financing. I enlisted the help of family members and combined this with a few no-money-down strategies. Before long, I had purchased my first 20+ properties. I had a great sense of accomplishment with each deal. I knew I was on the right track to success and fulfilling my lifelong dream of being an entrepreneur.

The first properties that I purchased were Section 8 rentals (subsidized housing). Once I figured out how to buy properties, fix them up and resell them without my own money I was unstoppable. I started doing this and I saw my financial worth and my confidence soar! I was making more on one deal than most people make in a month. From time to time, I would come across a few deals where the owner was willing to finance the properties for me. I didn't have to rely on anyone's credit and I didn't need cash, as the deals came fast.

Early on I learned not to be narrow-minded when it comes to real estate deals. To make money you have to understand that each situation is unique and may call for different strategies and priorities. Variables that affect my deals include: the seller's situation, my resources and risk tolerance, and the state of the actual property. This discovery taught me to look at each deal from different angles in order to optimize the potential. That allowed me to determine the best strategy to get into deals with no money down, while still keeping my sellers satisfied, and it put big money in my pocket. After handling hundreds of transactions I had reached a point of incredible success in my real estate career.

As I stated at the beginning of this report, I've made a lot of money, and I've also lost a lot of money in this business. If you're interested in pursuing a career in real estate investing, you must be ready for failure. It's the only way that you will learn and my case is no different. My goal is to help you minimize mistakes that will cost you money, prepare you to handle your future deals, especially the potentially bad ones that may come your way.

Trouble came my way when the market crashed. I lost a handful of properties due to declining values and low interest from buyers. I was one of the lucky ones because I had liquidated many properties before this happened because I had already planned to transition into bigger multi-family/apartment complex deals.

My dream eventually became a nightmare as it came crashing down around me, and I lost everything that I had worked so hard to attain. I made a series of mistakes that ended up devastating my financial situation and my confidence. I eventually lost everything I had to move from my beautiful 2800 square foot house with a pool. My new residence was a small one-bedroom apartment that was literally in the ghetto. It was so similar to where I grew up I wondered if my success had been some sort of dream, or even worse a fluke.

I spent a year trying to figure out how I got back to where I started. This was a time of self-doubt, depression, and frustration. I felt paralyzed by my losses but I refused to let bad circumstances triumph over me and vowed that I would be successful once more. I decided to gather myself up and get back to what I do best -- make money!

The very moment that I made the decision to take action I received IMMEDIATE results.

Here's what happened:

I stepped out of my humble apartment and started driving around. While I was driving aimlessly I came across a "For Sale by Owner" property. I stopped and called the owner, and my life was changed once more. I made a deal with the owner to buy not just one but four properties from him. I sold the four properties at wholesale prices to an investor and this was the first step of my comeback. I didn't need any money or credit because I didn't have to take ownership of those properties. The owner and I agreed on a price and I locked the deal up with a contract. I sold two of the properties within two weeks, and I had all four sold within a month. My profit from these 4 properties was $20,000 total, and this was just for one month of work.

From that point on I never looked back. Real estate is truly the only business I know where you can get into a deal with negative dollars in your bank account and within a matter of weeks you can make this kind of money. If I can do this, anyone can. I did not have a lot of experience, money, or training when I started in 2002. Anyone can be successful if they have enough drive and they are willing to learn and work hard. My parents taught me this lesson and it is one I believe in wholeheartedly.

My hope is to reach as many people as possible with my story. I want to inspire and motivate others to succeed, by giving them the tools they need to pursue their dreams and live a fulfilling life. Everyone deserves a life that they will love. That is my wish!

Sandy Cesaire

"Teaching You How To Turn Your Obstacles Into Opportunities"

More books by Sandy Cesaire from Sandycesaire.com

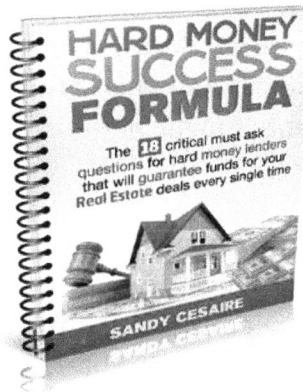